HYPERWAVE THEORY

THE ROGUE WAVES OF FINANCIAL MARKETS

D. TYLER JENKS, TYLER D. COATES, AND LEAH WALD

ARCHWAY PUBLISHING

Archway Publishing books may be ordered through booksellers or by contacting:

Archway Publishing
1663 Liberty Drive
Bloomington, IN 47403
www.archwaypublishing.com
1 (888) 242-5904

Because of the dynamic nature of the Internet, any web addresses or links contained in this book may have changed since publication and may no longer be valid. The views expressed in this work are solely those of the author and do not necessarily reflect the views of the publisher, and the publisher hereby disclaims any responsibility for them.

Any people depicted in stock imagery provided by Getty Images are models, and such images are being used for illustrative purposes only.
Certain stock imagery © Getty Images.

ISBN: 978-1-4808-8876-0 (sc)
ISBN: 978-1-4808-8877-7 (e)

Library of Congress Control Number: 2020903606

Print information available on the last page.

Archway Publishing rev. date: 2/29/2020

CONTENTS

ACKNOWLEDGEMENTS

Dearest Hyperwavers, thank you for creating a beautiful community of support, collaboration, and education. This book would not be possible without you.

Tone, thank you for believing in us and helping us navigate the Wild West of Bitcoin.

Gabriel Harber, thank you for helping to edit the final draft of the manuscript.

And to the talented photographer and friend Daisy Komen, thank you for taking our author photos. You encapsulated Tyler's spirit with your photograph where he can forever be a Bitcoin Standard Bearer.

This book is dedicated to Tyler Jenks, our co-author, who passed away on July 23, 2019.

Tyler spent his entire professional career studying financial markets and investments. He loved to share his extensive experience and investment acumen through classes, seminars, and the financial media. He will always be loved, remembered, and missed.

Tyler invented and developed hyperwave theory during the massive run-up in commodities that occurred in the 1970s. He implemented this newfound approach to sell silver in the low to mid $30s in 1980, less than a month before Silver Thursday.

One year later, he noticed a very similar pattern forming in the US long-term interest rates, which had skyrocketed from 5 percent to over 15 percent in fifteen years. In 1982, Tyler published a twenty-five-page article entitled "The Case for Bonds," and he called for rates to return to 6 percent when they were still above 12 percent.

That call was entirely due to hyperwave theory, and it allowed him to predict what few others could believe at that time. It also allowed him to make a very valuable inference: a long phase 7 in interest rates should result in a long bull market in equities. Dwindling interest rates are generally very bullish for equities, and this induction allowed him to build heavy, long exposure in the S&P 500 in 1983 when the price was in the $150 neighborhood.

He proceeded to use his new theory to sell the S&P 500 and Dow Jones Industrial Average in October 1987, one week before Black Monday. At that time, the S&P was $311.12, and D. Tyler made more than a 100 percent ROI in less than five years by narrowly avoiding the record-breaking crash that followed.

His most lucrative investment was right around the corner, as was the best call of his career. The Japanese equity market was forming the largest hyperwave that the world has ever known, returning over 4,000 percent in less than twenty years. The peak was at 39,270, and Tyler sold at slightly under 35,000. He proceeded to call for a return to the mid four digits, which was almost inconceivable at the time. The Lost Decade followed, and prices fell below five figures right as Tyler was in the process of selling the top of his fourth bubble.

The dot-com bubble that formed in the 1990s sent the Nasdaq into a beautiful hyperwave. The last five years of the millennium were the biggest returns that the US stock market had ever experienced; however, most were unable to capitalize on the run-up.

Some stayed out entirely; others became overexposed at or near the top and were confronted with huge losses after the market reversed.

Tyler focused on buying growth stocks during the mid-1990s when the Nasdaq was still below $500. The hyperwave became apparent shortly thereafter, and by this point, he had tremendous confidence in his ability to trade the pattern. Around this time, he was promoted to chief investment officer at Amivest Capital Management, but he was severely restricted in how he could manage money. The maximum cash allocation allowed was 5 percent. When the Nasdaq broke down phase 4, he was handcuffed but was still able to rotate out of growth stocks and into value. His performance led PS Ephron to rank him in the 99th percentile of money managers from 1998 to 2003.

Hyperwaves became much less common over the following decade; however, his best trade was still on the horizon. His son called at the beginning of 2017 and said that he thought Bitcoin was starting a hyperwave. Tyler looked at the charts and agreed with his son's analysis. He entered his entire retirement account in GBTC (the Bitcoin Investment Trust) that summer at an average cost basis of $3,200. He sold in December 2017 at $12,500 for nearly a 400 percent ROI in less than six months. He went on to project that Bitcoin would return to phase 1, which is waiting at $1,000.

Many people will make calls and predictions while very few are willing to put their entire retirement account at risk. Tyler made bold calls, and he made even bolder trades. His best calls and trades had all been a direct result of hyperwave theory.

This book will dive deep into the theory that took Tyler a lifetime to develop. We will show exactly how Tyler was able to sell the top of the most prominent bubbles that have occurred over the past forty years, and we will provide a complete strategy that will allow readers to repeat this process. There are currently more active hyperwaves than there have ever been in recorded history; therefore, hyperwave theory has never been more important. We will explore how to profit from these patterns, and we will delve into the macroeconomic repercussions of these financial rogue waves that are currently swelling in unprecedented proportions.

We are eternally grateful to Tyler for his love and support as a partner, mentor, and friend. He will never be forgotten as he will remain in our hearts forever.

PHASE 1

TECHNICAL THEORY

CHAPTER 1

TECHNICAL THEORY & HYPERWAVE ARCHETYPE

All through time, people have basically acted and reacted the same way
in the market as a result of greed, fear, ignorance, and hope. That is why
the numerical formations and patterns recur on a constant basis.

—Jesse Livermore

People familiar with financial markets are likely very familiar with the different types of chart patterns that are prevalent, including head and shoulders, double tops, triangles, wedges, etc. Even if one does not understand or believe in the implications of these patterns, one is likely aware that they recur constantly.

It is easy to conclude that a chart pattern is nothing more than a coincidence or a self-fulfilling prophecy; however, we prefer a far more nuanced view and remain intrigued by the idea that patterns are a manifestation of collective emotions.

When bears growl and bulls charge, the spirits of these animals permeate into society and affect the way that we think and act. This is when we can make irrational decisions because finance is not exempt from wild emotional extremes. Contrariwise, it is a reflection of the collective consciousness of all participants.

Irrational exuberance can easily be seen by examining the classic historical bubble case examples of the tulip mania, the South Sea bubble, the Great Depression, the dot-com bubble, and the mortgage crisis.

History doesn't repeat itself; emotions do.

The feelings of greed, fear, ignorance, and hope are the same regardless of skin color, nationality, gender, age, or calendar year. When participating in the markets with an expectation of making profit, we feel the same emotions as our ancestors. The patterns we see in today's financial markets are a representation of these collective emotions; therefore, they should remain essentially unchanged throughout space and time.

Head and shoulders patterns occurred in the early 1900s just as they occur now. Furthermore, they are just as prevalent in Japan, China, Germany, and other parts of Europe as they are in the United States.

Tyler developed the proprietary technical system of hyperwave in 1979. Hyperwave can be characterized as a chart pattern, but it is also much more than that. Hyperwave is a social phenomenon, and it is an expression of a macroeconomic shift. On a psychological level, hyperwave is a simple model to explain what happens when people refuse to allow the numbers to add up.

Macroeconomic shifts are extremely rare; therefore, so are hyperwaves. We are currently experiencing more hyperwaves than at any other point in recorded history, so we are likely undergoing the largest macroeconomic shift that has ever occurred.

When the dot-com bubble finally collapsed, everyone was shocked and embarrassed at how oblivious, misled, misinformed, and stupid they had been. Approximately 95 percent of the companies went to $0, and almost everyone was completely wiped out. These were not stupid people; they just acted stupid because of irrational exuberance.

The system cleansed itself.

The system always cleanses itself.

And after the correction, the great bull market ensued.

A historical doppelgänger appeared again with the mortgage crisis. The Federal Reserve, Congress, and the banking industry all created policies whereby mortgages were ridiculously available to ridiculously unqualified buyers. This accelerated from 2003 to 2007. Then the house of cards came crashing down.

In both cases, the collateral damage was catastrophic.

This was because so many were swept up by the hype and so few were looking at the bigger picture. It does not matter how smart you are. It has nothing to do with intelligence. The takeaway here is that it is human nature and emotions often supersede rationality and intellect.

All hyperwaves have common characteristics. The trademark is irrational exuberance that results from a macroeconomic shift, such as the invention of the internet or railroad. Nevertheless, each will have their own unique qualities.

Hyperwaves are like snowflakes in the way that they are created. Snowflakes form in a seemingly haphazard way. Two points form over here and one over there. There is no such thing as identical snowflakes; however, they all form into nearly identical structures. This is exactly how hyperwaves take shape.

It is important to understand that hyperwave is not dependent on price, whereas most other technical indicators are, such as moving averages, stochastic oscillator, moving average convergence divergence (MACD), or the TD Sequential. All those indicators need a price input to provide an output.

Hyperwave tells us exactly what pattern the price will follow before the move even begins. A hyperwave has seven phases, and before one forms, this is what it will look like before it ends:

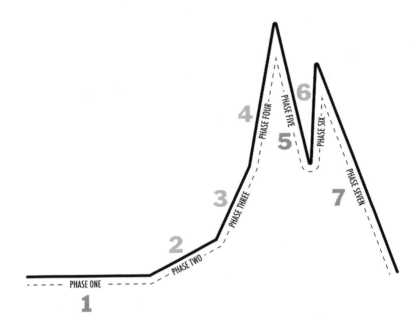

The Hyperwave Archetype

Many technical indicators will help to predict the direction of price movement, and others will help to forecast the duration.

Hyperwave is the only technical system that projects the pattern. Hyperwave does not provide a price target for phase 4, and it does not tell you how long it will take to get there. Limitations can be deduced through studying many hyperwaves. That can provide a roadmap for the duration and amplitude of certain phases but since each hyperwave is unique we can only make loose inductions from studying past limitations.

The vertices that separate each phase are the variables that distinguish hyperwave from parabolic theory. A vertex is a point; it is not an area. It is one point between two lines that determines the next movement of price in such a way that when the vertex occurs, price is going to respect the lines that are drawn in between the vertices.

Phase 1 is an elongated period of inaction. Phase 2 begins with a penetration upward of the phase 1 line. And price moves continually upward at a phase 2 angle. Phase 3 is the point at which a hyperwave is born. Phase 4 is the final acceleration at a very steep angle where prices are pushed to unsustainable levels. Phases 5, 6, and 7 are all bear market phases with Phase 6 being a countertrend bounce in a bear market.

From a technical analysis perspective, the basic structure will do two things. Firstly, phases 1, 5, and 7 will be ceilings above which price refuses to rise. Secondly, phases 2, 3, 4, and 6 are floors below which price refuses to fall.

The structure is predetermined before the price begins to rise. It is only after we draw the third and fourth phases that we will know the angle/shape a particular hyperwave (snowflake) will form.

A first-dimensional object has length only—no width or depth—and this provides the essence of a hyperwave. It is similar to a first-dimensional object in that it is a series of lines that have been drawn to connect the most important points within the system. It has only shape and is independent of price or time.

Hyperwave is a specific type of bubble. This book will explore how to capitalize on the abundant amount of hyperwaves that are currently active, and it will delve into the underlying fundamentals that are their driving force. We will also begin to explore the ramifications of breaking down phase 4 and entering the prolonged bear market, which is expected to retrace back to phase 1.

Our goal is to teach readers how to trade hyperwaves, but we also want to begin a discourse about how to minimize the fallout as it relates to the overall economy. Hyperwaves are like rogue waves in that they form due to a culmination of an underlying storm, can cause massive destruction, and completely disappear shortly thereafter. The only way to defend ourselves is through education, dialogue, and an open mind.

The current environment is not unique. There was another time, about ninety years ago, when an inordinate amount of hyperwaves swelled simultaneously. They collectively broke down phase 4 during the same period in 1929, and this resulted in the Great Depression. We do not point out this corollary to scare readers into thinking that the sky is falling. Instead, we hope to use historical examples to shed light onto our current macroeconomic environment as a way to prepare for, and potentially mitigate, the fallout that we believe is coming in the next few decades.

CHAPTER 2

TYPES OF BUBBLES

It is very important to note that all hyperwaves are bubbles, but not all bubbles are hyperwaves. There are many types of bubbles, the most common of which are parabolas, blow-off tops, deformed hyperwaves, and actual hyperwaves.

Blow-Off Top

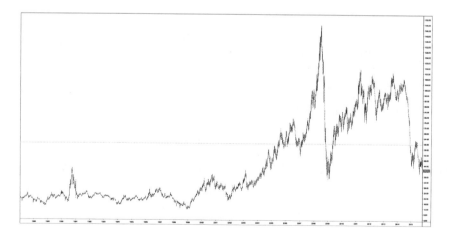

Blow-Off Top in West Texas Oil

Oil experienced a bubble in 2008; however, it should not be mistaken for a hyperwave. We view this as a blow-off top and would not expect any of the hyperwave rules to apply.

Parabola

The Russian Ruble

A hyperwave could be quantified as a parabolic advance; however, that is usually a mischaracterization. When technical analysts refer to a parabolic advance, curve, and/ or arc, they are usually referring to a rounded trend line.

For a hyperwave, the phase lines are always linear trend lines, and they are never curved.

Trading Litecoin with the rules of hyperwave in 2017 would have worked out very nicely; however, that does not necessarily imply that it was a hyperwave.

The further one gets away from the archetype, the more one is forced to make exceptions, or manipulations, to the rules. The more exceptions that are made, the less likely the price is to respect the rules and boundary lines. Conversely, the more perfected the pattern is, the higher the probability that it will complete each phase as expected.

Deformed Hyperwave

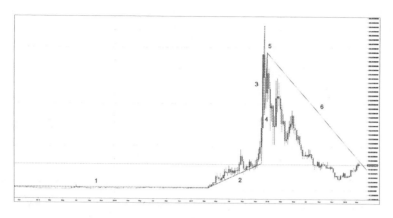

Litecoin

Figure 4: Litecoin

Hyperwaves have seven phases. Litecoin looks a lot like a hyperwave; however, there is no phase 3. Skipping the third phase only leaves us with six phases; therefore, it is not a hyperwave. It is a good impostor, but the lack of seven phases means that it is outside the realm of what can be considered a hyperwave.

Hyperwave

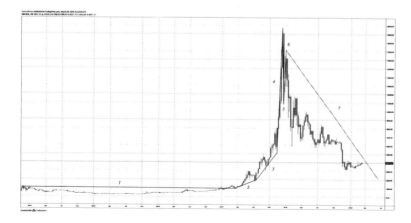

Bitcoin Hyperwave

The massive bull run that Bitcoin experienced during 2017 was a hyperwave. For this example, linear trend lines are a much better fit than a parabola. It is distinct from a blow-off top because of the fifth and sixth phases. This is because phase 5 starts when the weekly candle closes below phase 4. Phase 6 is the dead cat bounce that follows and creates a lower high. Blow-off tops do not have this bounce. Instead, they fully retrace the run-up in one swift move down.

Bitcoin also has seven phases, which distinguishes it from Litecoin. Therefore, Bitcoin fits the hyperwave archetype whereas the other three examples do not.

In the following sections, we will compare buying and holding versus timing the market, combating emotions when learning how to trade, and then we will provide a brief introduction to technical analysis (TA). These sections are meant for individuals who are new to active buying and selling as well as those who are new to TA. If you already have a firm grasp on these topics, then feel free to skip forward to "Psychology of Hyperwaves."

CHAPTER 3

INTRODUCTION TO TECHNICAL ANALYSIS

Hyperwave theory relies on the premise that it is possible to beat the market rate of return over a statistically significant sample size through the understanding and implementation of technical analysis (TA).

The large majority of investors do not believe that this is possible and as a result commit to indefinitely buying and holding. We believe that hyperwaves are the perfect example of why that approach is flawed. As we will learn later in this text, when bubbles burst, they go back to the area where they started.

We have seen this time and time again across all asset classes and time periods. Buying and holding means forgoing all potential profits and riding it back down to the bottom. Numerous strategies are repeatable and have been proven to outperform the buy-and-hold approach.

A primary objective of this book is to dispel that approach by showing how Tyler was able to buy near the bottom and sell near the top of every major market bubble since 1980. This includes, but is not limited to, silver in 1980, the Japanese asset bubble in 1990, the dot-com bubble in 2000, the mortgage crisis in 2008, and Bitcoin in December 2017.

Tyler was only able to accomplish this through his expertise in technical analysis and, more specifically, hyperwave theory.

While Warren Buffett gained notoriety for avoiding the dot-com bubble entirely, Tyler began to establish himself inside the top 1 percent of money managers in the world after selling yet another top.

Technical analysis is a very expansive, nuanced, and controversial field of study. Fortunately, there are only a couple of basic concepts that a reader needs to grasp to recognize and trade or invest in hyperwaves. Other advanced technical indicators can complement this pattern, and they will be discussed later in this book; however, they are not a necessity.

The section below is for individuals who are brand new to the concepts of TA. We will provide a brief overview of candlesticks, trend lines, moving averages, and areas of support and resistance.

Candlesticks

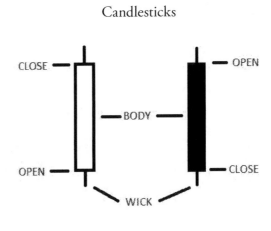

Candlesticks

There are several ways to view a chart. The most common is with a line, bars, or candlesticks. We will only cover candlesticks for this book because that is our preferred method when analyzing hyperwaves.

Candlestick charts were developed in Japan during the eighteenth century and were popularized by Steve Nison in the book *Japanese Candlestick Charting Techniques*[1]. A rice trader by the name of Munehisa Homma is credited by most as the creator; however, Mr. Nison speculates that candlesticks were first concocted at an earlier time period[2].

What is crucial to understand for the purposes of this book is identifying where the candle opens and closes as well as how to distinguish and interpret the wicks. Candles can be used on any time frame from one minute to more than a year. Hyperwave is only concerned with weekly candles, and that is the time frame that we will be using by default. If it is a different time frame, then we will be sure to clarify.

In traditional markets, a weekly candle opens on Monday and closes on Friday. This is represented by the body of the candle. If the candle is green, then that means it opened at the bottom of the body and closed at the top. If the candle is red, then it opened at the top of the body and closed at the bottom. In a black and white environment, the green candles are white and red candles are black (as in the picture below).

Bar charts are a more traditional form of visualizing the Open-High-Low-Close (OHLC) and they were the standard for years. Candles only became popular in the last two to three decades. What is most important is being able to accurately draw trendlines and identify the weekly close. We prefer candlesticks but bars, or even line charts, are perfectly acceptable.

A wick appears if the asset briefly traded at those prices but failed to close in that area. A wick below a green candle tells us that price fell slightly after opening but rallied strongly throughout the rest of the period and closed higher than the open.

A wick below the red (black) candle represents price falling to that area at some point in the period and then making a rebound before closing above the lows while remaining below the open.

---

[1] Nison, Steve, *Japanese Candlestick Charting Techniques, Second Edition.*
[2] Nison, Steve, *Beyond Candlesticks: New Japanese Charting Techniques Revealed*

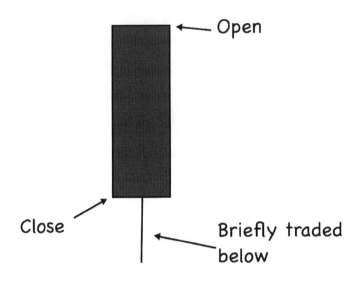

Candle

When analyzing hyperwaves, we prefer to use candlesticks for several reasons. The most important is being able to distinguish between a close and a wick.

Hyperwave theory states that when a weekly candle closes below a trend line, then the top is in. However, there will be countless examples where the price falls below the trend line on an intraweek basis before it eventually closes above. This is illustrated with a wick below the trend line followed by a close above.

Wicks below Phase 4 Trend Line

In the image above, we can see a candle opening below the phase 4 trend line (#1) followed by a wick that takes the price even further below the trend line (# 2) before it proceeds to close above the all-important threshold (#3). All are acceptable, and the phase remains intact as long as the *weekly* candle closes above the trend line.

Later we see multiple wicks go below the trend line and again fail to close under that area of support (#4).

Support and Resistance

Support is a barrier that holds the price above it. Conversely, resistance holds price below. Both can be identified by using various technical indicators, the most common of which are horizontal trend lines, angular trend lines, and moving averages (MA).

Phase 1 is identified by a prolonged period when the price fails to close a weekly candle above a horizontal trend line. The horizontal trend line at the top of phase 1 is resistance. Supply will increase as the price approaches that area, and demand will simultaneously decrease.

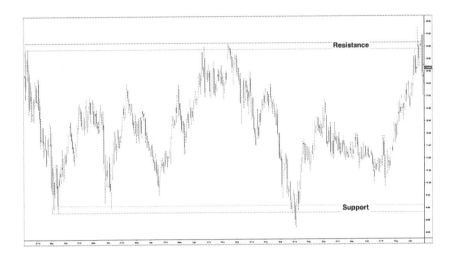

Support and Resistance

The opposite of resistance is support. If the price fails to break through resistance, then it will sell off until finding an area of support. The lower prices get increasingly attractive for buyers and less appealing for sellers. This will continue until it reaches a point where demand far exceeds supply. The horizontal movement that is illustrated in the chart above is referred to as a trading range.

A reliable rule of thumb is the following: the longer a price stays stuck in a trading range, the more explosive the following move is expected to be after support or resistance is broken.

This is primarily why we consider phase 1 to be the most important of all phases. Short phase 1's lead to smaller hyperwaves in terms of amplitude and duration. The longer a phase 1 lasts, the larger the resulting hyperwave is expected to be.

Another important rule of thumb is that resistance tends to become support after is violated, and the inverse is also true.

Resistance Turns into Support Following Breakthrough

Support Turning into Resistance

Support and resistance areas can be drawn with a line or as a zone/area. Both are perfectly valid.

Trend Lines

Trend lines are areas of support and resistance that are represented with horizontal or angular lines. If the trend line is horizontal, as are all phase 1 trend lines, then that represents a trading range and will usually come with a corresponding horizontal trend line for support.

Trend lines that are at an angle, such as phases 2–7, mark support or resistance in a trending market. A trend is the opposite of a range. Ranges move sideways, and trends move the price up or down. Bear trend lines occur when the price is declining, and bull trend lines occur when prices are increasing. Trend lines also represent the direction and velocity of the market.

The angle of the trend line in relation to the x-axis represents the velocity. The steeper the angle, the greater the velocity. The more gradual the angle, the slower it is moving and the closer it is to entering a trading range.

Bitcoin Bear Trend Line

S&P 500 Bull Trend Line

A trend line needs at least three touch points to be considered valid. The trend line is broken once a weekly candle closes below. It is okay to have wicks break the trend line, as long it closes above on a weekly time frame.

When there are both support and resistance trend lines, then this is considered a parallel channel.

Bitcoin Bear Parallel Channel

When a trend line is broken on a weekly closing basis, then it is a strong indication of the move becoming exhausted. After a trend becomes exhausted, it will often correct, reverse, or develop a range. A correction is generally seen as a healthy cool-off period before the trend resumes and can be considered the one step back after taking two forward.

Consider the S&P 500. It will often enter bull markets that last multiple years. Within that larger-scale bull run, there will be days, weeks, and months when the price declines. This is healthy. No markets go straight up or straight down, at least not for long. Corrections happen in both directions. In bear markets, the price will correct upward, and in bull markets, corrections will be downward.

A reversal occurs when the countertrend move completely reverses the trend. The years 2001 and 2008 were more than healthy corrections in the US stock markets; they were full-on reversals that turned a bull market into a bear market.

Being able to distinguish corrections from reversals is the single hardest part about technical analysis. Violating multiyear trend lines is a great way to do this. The best part about hyperwave theory is that it knows exactly how to identify reversals opposed to corrections. Very few other indicators or chart patterns have this capability.

Phase lines are trend lines that occur within a hyperwave. In this book, the term will be used synonymously, but keep in mind that all phase lines are trend lines but very few trend lines are phase lines. Hyperwaves and phase lines are very rare, whereas trend lines are always prevalent.

Moving Averages

Moving averages are very intuitive indicators for most. They are calculated just as one would expect: fifty-day moving average (MA) is derived by adding the closing price from the last fifty daily closes and then dividing by fifty. Each time a new candle closes, a new data point is plotted. A line connects these points and is overlaid on the chart.

This period can be adjusted, and that would mean that a different number of candles is being used in the calculation. Moving averages can be very useful for several reasons.

They are a very common and effective tool used to identify areas of support and resistance as well as to recognize trends.

In the good old days, technical indicators needed to be charted by hand and that was how Tyler Jenks started. He always strongly encouraged the other two co-authors to learn indicators by manually doing the calculations. Sure enough there are tremendous insights waiting for those who are willing to put in the effort. For example, how much does an extremely volatile day or two effect a 200-day MA? In general, it is not nearly as much as one would assume and realizing this will provide a much more nuanced view of how moving averages interact with the price.

Bitcoin Moving Average

The 50- and 200-day moving averages (MAs) are the most common, and for good reason. The chart above shows how well the 50 MA can identify areas of support and resistance. As we learned above, areas of resistance are likely to turn into support following a valid breakthrough.

Something else to pay close attention to is the angle of the moving average. This can be a very powerful tool for recognizing trends. When longer-term MAs are angled down, with the price below, that is indicative of a bear market. If angled upward, with the price above, then that is indicative of a bull trend. Flat MA's indicate a ranging market(s).

Moving averages are based entirely on math, which makes them objective. The best indicators eliminate gray areas while painting a black and white picture. Moving averages are the single best example of this concept, which is why the authors of this book have such an affinity for them.

There are numerous other ways to use MAs to stay one step ahead of the market, such as crossovers; however, that will need to be saved for another time and potentially another book. As a quick side note, Tyler Jenks also invented a system for trading moving averages that has been mathematically proven to consistently beat the market over long periods of time. That system is called Consensio and it is the primary tool that Tyler used to manage billions of dollars throughout his career.

Stop-Losses

If one decides that buying and holding is not the best approach, then it is very important to become adept with stop-losses. There are many tools that one can use to set and adjust stop-losses, including but not limited to moving averages, trend lines, parabolic SAR, and the Williams Fractal, developed by Bill Williams.

Successful trading hinges on two premises:

1. It is possible to beat the market's rate of return consistently and over a statistically significant sample size.
2. It is impossible to be right 100 percent of the time.

To expand on the second point, it is possible to consistently beat the markets while being wrong 50–75 percent of the time. This is possible through only entering trades with an asymmetrical risk: reward ratio. If winning trades net 50 percent and losing trades cost 10 percent, then one only needs to be right on one's positions >21 percent of the time to be profitable.

A trader needs to have a clear understanding of where his or her position falls apart and therefore when a stop-loss must be executed. For example, if buying an area of horizontal support, then price breaking down that area indicates a trade falling apart and a necessity for exiting the position before losses get out of control.

Risk management is vital to succeeding as a trader, investor, or buy-and-holder. Regardless of the strategy that one employs, it will be impossible to stay solvent for a statistically significant sample size without proper risk management. For traders, risk management hinges on the use of stop-losses and capital reserves. For investors and long-term holders, risk management mostly comes down to diversification and an emergency fund.

Regardless of how one decides to proceed after reading this book, it is vital to implement proper risk management techniques. Many different indicators can be used to better the market's returns; however, they all rely on sound risk management.

Not all technical indicators are created equally, and it is almost always preferable to use a combination of indicators when making a decision as opposed to blindly following one.

Therefore, it is very important to have a hierarchy of technical indicators so that one can begin to develop a feel for which works best in different circumstances. Think of this hierarchy as being analogous to a master carpenter's tool belt. Not only does he know what tools and materials will be needed to complete the job, as well as how much they cost, he also knows when to use them. On the other hand, a novice may not even know the name of an apparatus, let alone how or why it is used in different situations.

It takes thousands of hours to develop the nuanced view of an expert. That only comes through experience and training. Only through applying different indicators in different market conditions is it possible to begin developing one's hierarchy of indicators.

Once equipped with the right tools, it is possible to begin constructing an empire.

Hierarchy of Indicators

1. Hyperwave: created by D. Tyler Jenks
2. Consensio: created by D. Tyler Jenks
3. Coppock Curve: created by Edwin Sedge[3]

---

[3] The Coppock Curve was developed by E.S.C. Coppock and first published in Barron's Magazine on October 15, 1962

4. Other patterns: originally recognized and recorded by Jesse Livermore[4], John Magee, Robert Edwards[5], and Wallace Schabacker[6]
5. Horizontal support and resistance[7]
6. Trend lines
7. Candlesticks: created by Munehisa Homma
8. Parabolic SAR (parabolic stop and reverse): created by Welles Wilder[8]
9. TD Sequential: originally created by Larry Williams[9]; improved upon by Tom Demark and Tone Vays
10. Relative Strength Index (RSI): created by Welles Wilder
11. Average Directional Index (ADX): created by Welles Wilder

Hyperwave is currently at the top of the totem pole, but that distinction is usually reserved for Consensio. This is because Consensio can be used in all markets, at all times, whereas hyperwave is generally very rare. This adjustment is due to how many hyperwaves are currently active and is a great example of how the hierarchy is always being adjusted based on market conditions.

Once one starts to understand where certain indicators fall on the pecking order, the next step is to develop an understanding for when to move one up or down the totem pole. Trend lines and horizontals are other great examples. Horizontals are always more powerful than trend lines unless it is phase 2, 3, or 4 of a hyperwave. When the asset is in a hyperwave, the trend lines, or phase lines, become more important than horizontals.

---

[4] Livermore, J. (1940). *How to Trade In Stocks*. New York: Duell, Sloan and Pearce.

[5] Edwards, R. and Magee, J. (1948). *Technical Analysis of Stock Trends*. Springfield, MA: Stock Trend Service.

[6] Schabacker, R. (1930). *Technical analysis and stock market profits*. B. C. Forbes publishing company.

[7] Recommended books by Thomas Bulkowski on Horizontal Support and Resistence as well as trendlines include: 1) Chart Patterns: After the Buy, 2) Getting Started in Chart Patterns, 3) Trading Basics, 4) Fundamental Analysis and Position Trading: Evolution of a Trader, 5) Swing and Day Trading: Evolution of a Trader, 6) Visual Guide to Chart Patterns, 7) Encyclopedia of Chart Pattern.

[8] Wilder, J. (1978). *New concepts in technical trading systems*. Greensboro, N.C.: Trend Research. In this book, he also describes the Relative Strength Index (RSI) and the Average Directional Index (ADX) listed below.

[9] Williams, L. (1980). *Sequential "The Third Element of Thrust Dynamics"*. Communications Research.

In normal market conditions, hyperwaves are so rare that they can be removed from the hierarchy. A technical trading system loses a large part of its value if it can only be used a couple of times in someone's life. Does it really matter how well the rules of hyperwave work if there are no active hyperwaves?

Fortunately for everyone reading, that has never been further from the case than it is right now. There has never been another time in human history when this many hyperwaves were active.

The success rate of an indicator is largely defined by the number of signals it provides. When a system has an inordinately high success rate, then it is likely because the buy-and-sell signals are rare. If a very successful indicator starts to provide an abnormal amount of signals, then it is time to sit up in our seats and pay very close attention.

There are only a handful of logical inductions that one can make following the increased rate of buy-and-sell signals that are being generated.

1. The indicator is losing its effectiveness and is expected to provide more and more false signals, fakeouts, and/or traps moving forward.
2. It is the right place and the right time to make hay while the sun shines.

CHAPTER 4

BUYING AND HOLDING VERSUS TIMING THE MARKET

Financial markets exist as a way to transfer wealth from the anxious and emotional to the patient and rational. Anyone with experience in the markets has a deep understanding of the emotions that are inherent to speculating. This is why most make the seemingly rational choice of forgoing actively buying and selling in favor of buying and holding.

The prevailing logic is that it is impossible to beat the markets by attempting to time the reversals; therefore, the best strategy is to buy and hold a well-diversified portfolio of stocks, bonds, and commodities.

For many people, this is sound advice. The emotions of active buying and selling can be overwhelming. The anxiety and stress that result from this decision-making process often mean that the effort is not worth the reward.

Furthermore, finding a money manager with integrity who can consistently beat the markets is an extremely daunting task and can feel like trying to find a needle in a burning haystack.

While buying and holding may be the best approach for some people, specifically those who do not have the time or ability to beat the markets, it is not necessarily the best approach for everyone. This book relies on the premise that it is possible to consistently beat a buy-and-hold strategy through the use of technical and fundamental analysis as well as proper risk management.

If it was impossible to consistently better the market's return on investment (ROI), then hyperwave theory would be futile. Many individuals harbor life experience that has led them to eschew technical analysis (TA) as well as the idea that it is possible to time the markets.

If technical analysis does not produce favorable results for an individual or a small group over a defined time period, then it does not necessarily imply that the entire field of TA is invalid. It simply means that the individual or small group was incapable, unwilling, or uncommitted. Conversely, if a trading system can net positive results for a single individual over a long enough time, then it is valid.

Long enough is subjective and will have to be ascertained individually through backtesting the approach in different market conditions—flat, bull, bear, linear, and parabolic. The fact that the system can be backtested with the scientific method throughout space and time is exactly what confirms its validity.

Later in this book, we will explore a handful of indicators and patterns that are proven to dominate the market's average rate of return.

Many fall short of comprehending the power of technical analysis due to a lack of understanding of basic probability as well as the regressive memory bias, which believes that humans have a tendency to recall high probabilities lower than they actually were and vice versa.

Technical analysis does not work 100 percent of the time. If a trading system has a 60 percent success rate, then it will be very hard for the mind to believe that is true after a losing streak of more than ten trades in a row. Unless accompanied by a sufficient grasp of probability, it is natural for a person to believe that the success rate is much lower than 50 percent and that the creator of the system is a charlatan.

Now consider the fact that some of the world's most accomplished traders are wrong approximately 75 percent of the time. Not only is it possible to consistently better the returns of your favorite no-load mutual fund, but it is also possible to do so with an approximately 25 percent strike rate. Grasping this concept is vital because without such an understanding, it will be very difficult to conceptualize the intangibles of what it takes to consistently outperform the markets.

Beating the market with less than a 50% strike rate is possible through an even bigger imbalance in the risk: reward ratio. If 25 percent of the trades are winners and the minimum risk-reward requirement is 1:5, then it is possible to consistently turn a profit over the long run. If enough trades are executed throughout the year, then this will be enough to beat the market.

We assert that it is possible to time the markets, but we do not mean to imply that it is easy. Getting back up on a horse after it has repeatedly bucked you off is extremely difficult. It is exponentially more difficult after that same horse kicks you in the teeth.

A 25 percent to 50 percent success rate implies some very nasty losing streaks.

Those stretches will make you question your belief in your abilities, the system you are trading, and technical analysis as a whole. Even the most rational will likely fall victim to this thought process due to the regressive memory and egocentric biases.

Swing and position traders are much more vulnerable to this than day traders. That is because they have a longer time horizon and make fewer trades per year; therefore, they will take much longer to reach a point where the sample size is statistically significant. That is important because it is often the variable of time that has a larger psychological impact than the variable of volume, provided that the risk is similar.

To put it another way, it is easier to lose twenty consecutive trades in a week than it is to have fifteen consecutive losing trades over six months. Combined with human's preference for immediate gratification, this goes a long way to explain why there are so few swing and position traders compared to scalpers[10] and day traders.

Coping with these emotions and biases becomes exponentially more challenging if there is an audience.

---

[10] A scalp trade or "scalping" is a trading style that takes small profit positions from minor changes in intra-day small stock price changes. Positions can be held from seconds to minutes and often scalpers carry out hundreds of trades during an average trading day.

When nothing seems to be working the way it should is exactly when the naysayers will come out of the woodwork, whether they be family, friends, clients, fans, or critics. They will be impatiently waiting to question your ability and intelligence, especially if their previous life experience or education led them to conclude that it is impossible to time the market.

This is where most will capitulate and pass on the next buy or sell that his or her voodoo trading system signals. Inevitably that will be the signal that works and is intended to make up for a large majority, if not all, of the prior losses. Most trading strategies rely on 10–20 percent of the positions to return 80–90 percent of the profits. Missing one trade could turn a profitable year into a loser.

Fortunately, there is one very effective tool for managing emotions when trading for the first time or trying out a new system. We have found it to work time and time again across all asset classes and personality types.

Start small.

To combat the emotions and stress that are inherent to trading and investing we strongly urge inexperienced individuals to gain experience through *starting small.*

Approximately 95 percent of the mental anguish that is experienced by new traders/investors can be eliminated by decreasing position size. Many will think they are taking this advice by cutting their position in half, and that is not true. If you notice that the emotions are affecting your decision-making, then we implore you to decrease your position by at least 90 percent.

Starting with an amount that one is comfortable with losing is the best way to learn how to trade. If you have $1,000 set aside to trade, then consider starting with $10. That takes a huge weight off one's shoulders, which is very important when the appendages are not battle hardened. Removing that weight is what will allow you to focus on what matters. That one step will provide a big edge over the majority who are blinded by greed, fear, hope, and ignorance.

The immediate reaction will usually be something along the lines of "Ten dollars is not going to generate any sort of meaningful return," and that is precisely the point.

The most important part is gaining experience and learning from mistakes that everyone makes. Focus on building a track record of proven returns that are greater than the indices. Instead of thinking about the dollar amount that is being returned, it is important to consider the return on investment (ROI) in relation to the time that it took to generate.

Think Big

After utilizing this strategy enough that you have a statistically significant sample size, then you are in a position to start betting bigger and making meaningful projections. The key is to establish a reliable track record such that you will have the experience needed to persevere through the long downswings. Being able to manage risk and stay resilient during downswings are the most important determinants of long-term success. Through starting small and thinking big, it is possible to gain this experience without putting a significant amount of money at risk.

Tax Considerations

Most of the investing world falls into two categories.

- those who believe it is impossible to time the market; therefore, it is best to buy and hold
- those who believe that tax obligations from actively buying and selling are far too cumbersome to overcome; therefore, it is best to buy and hold

Both of those conclusions are faulty. The first line of thinking is by far the most common and a significant part of this book has been dedicated to dispelling that notion. After one opens one's eyes to the possibility of timing the market with technical analysis, then one often assumes that short-term capital gains render active buying and selling untenable. This section will attempt to allay the latter assumption.

Let's use Bitcoin as an example to mathematically prove the absurdity of neglecting profit-taking due to a misunderstanding of tax implications. By implementing the rules of hyperwave, Tyler was able to enter GBTC at $3,200 and exit at $12,500. This occurred in less than one year and was therefore subject to short-term capital gains.

Let us assume that his exposure was $1,000,000.

$12,500/$3,200 = 3.90/390 percent ROI.
$1,000,000 X 390 percent = $3,900,000.
Profit = $2,900,000.

Short-term capital gains are taxed up to 37%[11].

The capital gains in this scenario are $2,900,000.
$2,900,000 X 0.37 = $1,073,000 tax obligation.
$2,900,000 - $1,073,000 = $1,827,000 net profit.

Accounting for taxes, Tyler's 390% ROI becomes a 282.7% ROI.

Holding onto the position would indeed have shown a higher ROI *on paper* because it would not have accounted for the tax implications. However, unrealized profit is very different from the realized profit. The former is likely to disappear if given enough time, and the latter remains intact regardless of what happens to the price down the road.

Short-term capital gains are only applied to investments that are bought and sold in the same fiscal year. Let's assume that Tyler decided to wait for the one-year deadline to exit his position, under the premise that he wanted to pay fewer taxes by only subjecting himself to long-term capital gains.

Let's continue to use $1,000,000 in exposure
Enter $3,200 on August 7, 2017.
Exit at $6,695 on August 7, 2018.

$6,695/$3,200 = 2.09/209%.
$1,000,000 X 290% = $2,092,187.
Profit = $1,092,187.

Long-term capital gains are taxed up to 20%.[1]

---

[11] *Briefing Book - How are Capital Gains Taxed?* (2018). Retrieved from https://www.taxpolicycenter.org/briefing-book/how-are-capital-gains-taxed

The capital gains in this scenario are $1,092,187.
$1,092,187 X 0.2 = $218,437 tax obligation.
$1,092,187 - $218,437 = $873,749 net profit.

This is an example of when paying more in taxes means making more in profit. This is how taxes generally work and this is a common misconception.

Taking profit when the technicals demanded led to a tax obligation that was almost 500% more than it would have been if he waited to pay long-term capital gains—$218,437 versus $1,073,000. Despite the higher tax rate and having more to claim, the net profit was still more than twice as much—$873,749 versus $1,827,000.

People who use taxes as a reason to buy and hold indefinitely often focus on the tax obligation while forgetting to consider the net profit after taxes are paid. Those people are effectively arguing that it is better to have a smaller net profit since it results in a smaller sum of taxes being paid.

This is an absurd conclusion. At the end of the day, the net profit is all that matters. If making $1,000,000 entails paying $370,000 in taxes, then that is always better than making $500,000 and only paying $100,000 in taxes. It is better for the individual and better for the overall economy.

This shows that paying more in taxes does not necessarily mean making fewer profits. In fact, it is often the exact opposite. The more one pays in taxes, the more that person is usually netting at the end of the day. Individuals who focus on the amount paid in taxes over actual profit taken home have a flawed thought process.

After realizing that it is possible to time the markets, then it is important to realize that it is possible to better the average market returns despite tax consequences.

CHAPTER 5

PSYCHOLOGY OF HYPERWAVES

Hyperwaves start with a macroeconomic shift, and they progress mainly due to psychological factors. They are an expression of the collective emotions every market participant is experiencing.

A chart titled "The Wall Street Cheat Sheet: Psychology of a Market Cycle" is the most concise and comprehensive summary of the emotions that are experienced throughout different phases of an exponential market advance. This chart has price as the y-axis and time as the x-axis and explains each emotion felt as the market fluctuates and creates a bubble. These emotions are synonymous with every type of bubble, whether it is a hyperwave, a blow-off top, a parabolic advance, or some other deformity. Regardless of market structure, there will be euphoria at the top, anxiety, and denial on the way down, which is followed by panic, capitulation, depression, anger, and disbelief at the bottom.

If one is familiar with "The Wall Street Cheat Sheet[12]," then it could be easy to discount hyperwave as unoriginal at best or a complete rip-off at worst. The chart illustrates some of the emotions that repeat themselves in every bubble cycle, whereas hyperwave is a trading system that provides a set of rules for how to consistently profit from a specific subset of bubbles. The two should not be confused because one can help market participants to understand the emotions that are prevalent as the cycle progresses and the other is a set of rules that enables one to consistently capitalize on the repeating cycle.

---

[12] Wall Street Cheat Sheet: Psychology of a Market Cycle. Available at https://www.wallstcheatsheet.com

Hyperwave also delves into the socioeconomic implications of these recurring cycles. Thus far all hyperwaves have returned to phase 1, and that type of fluctuation can devastate entire economies. While the micro-effects are illustrated in the chart, we do not believe the descriptions outlined provide a sufficient explanation for the macroeconomic effects that are felt on a wider scale.

We remain thoroughly convinced that the presence of so many hyperwaves is a serious problem. The main reason is that they do not represent sustainable growth. Sustainable growth happens with two steps forward and one step back. It does not happen by leaping forward without looking back.

Hyperwaves do not add value to society. Once entering phase 4, they have historically returned to phase 1, and that causes exponentially more poverty than prosperity before the cycle is complete.

When everything is going well industry wide, it is easy to exaggerate strengths and believe that the music will continue indefinitely. However, being successful in a down market necessitates a more creative and crafty approach.

If this book is successful, then the readers will be able to prosper greatly from the record number of hyperwaves that are currently active. As Warren Buffet said:

"It's only when the tide goes out that you learn who has been swimming naked."

We hope that this book will prepare readers with proper attire for the low tide that is ahead.

Cognitive Dissonance

Cognitive dissonance and hyperwaves are kissing cousins. It's almost as if hyperwaves developed as a way to exploit the delusions that humans have evolved to identify with.

For better or worse, we are all biased toward our own benefit and making decisions for utility maximization, whether it be an egocentric bias that makes us remember that the fish was 25–50% bigger than it was or the confirmation bias that only seeks information to further corroborate prior beliefs.

If it wasn't for these innate dispositions and emotions that color our perceptions and actions the financial markets would cease to exist. If everyone always acted rationally, then would there be any room for speculation?

We do not believe there would be any place for speculative markets in a completely rational world. Markets exist as a way to transfer wealth from the emotional and irrational to the patient and disciplined. As long as people are willing to make irrational and suboptimal decisions as it relates to their savings and investments, then the speculative markets will continue to separate them from their wealth. It is simple. Price action responds to emotions.

That is true in all market conditions. It does not take a hyperwave to cause irrational decision-making; however, we believe that hyperwaves are the most proficient method of achieving this goal.

The two most common emotions felt in the bull market phase are greed and fear of missing out. Hyperwaves are so effective at exploiting these emotions that phase 4 will make it appear like the biggest risk a person could take is staying out or scaling out of the market.

Due to this phenomenon, the long-term holders become increasingly less willing to sell and the risk-averse become increasingly willing to buy. Even though the former stands to profit enormously, the potential of missing out on the next big move to the upside outweighs the prospect of capitalizing on profit.

Conversely, the latter group has decided to stay away throughout all of phase 2 and phase 3. This can be extremely difficult, depending on how long that person's friends, family, news outlets, or financial advisor have been telling them to get in. In phase 4, the perceived risk of staying out will start to overwhelm their perceived risk of entering late, and that will trap many in at exactly the wrong time.

Risk-averse buyers entering late is the inverse of panic sellers capitulating at the bottom. The former group was resolved to stay out of the market, and the latter group was determined to stay in. We believe that maximizing punishment for both groups is one of the, if not *the,* primary reasons why hyperwaves take the shape that they do.

Greed and fear of missing out will slowly turn into complacency as the market goes through the fifth and sixth phases.

Suddenly that will begin turning into anxiety, denial, and blind hope as the seventh phase takes control. Even though most longer-term holders are still in the green during the beginning and middle stages of phase 7, their delusions are so overwhelming that few consider selling when lower prices are realized.

As phase 7 continues, more and more of the longer-term holders become underwater on their positions. Now a new set of emotions is beginning to take over. The blind hope that many clung to becomes fleeting and is slowly replaced with anger.

Media outlets are reporting how much the asset is down in the last fiscal year. These are the same talking heads who told you to buy big only a few months or years earlier.

Friends and family are starting to ask what is going on.

"You told me to buy Bitcoin. What is going on with it?"

"You are still in Bitcoin?!" I just heard on the news that it is dead and is going to $0!"

Now market participants are being controlled by an entirely new set of emotions that further ensures rational decision-making will remain out of reach. Hope turns into anger. Anxiety becomes panic before turning into capitulation.

Now there are long-term holders' panic selling the bottom at a loss. These are the same individuals who chose to hold through phases 4, 5, and 6 when there was enormous unrealized profit on the table. These individuals could have also sold at some point in phase 7, admitting that they missed the top while still being able to capitalize on some profit.

For one emotion or another, the large majority of market participants lose money, and that is how you know the hyperwave achieved its goal.

There is something specific about hyperwave that accomplishes this goal better than any other pattern, and we would like to better understand why.

Deciding to buy, sell, or hold is largely a battle between incentive salience and associative learning.

Incentive salience deals with the underlying motivation of an individual by questioning what end that person hopes to attain when deciding to buy, sell, or hold.

Associative learning primarily deals with positive or negative reinforcement and the classical conditioning that was demonstrated with Pavlov's dog. This should be broken down into three categories, because each option prompts very different emotions/conditioning.

Deciding to Buy/Enter

On the surface, the motivating factors appear to fall into a relatively simple spectrum. On one end is an ambition to profit; on the other end is a desire to preserve.

Financial markets tend to transfer wealth from those trying to create it to those who are primarily concerned with preserving it. Individuals who are primarily motivated by creating new wealth are exponentially more susceptible to the emotions of greed and fear of missing out (emotions relating to bull markets).

Individuals who are primarily motivated by preserving wealth will be much more vulnerable to panic and anxiety (emotions related to bear market). The difference in emotions is a function of impetus. This is a concept that is crucial to understand. Every market participant will feel the same emotions at various stages of the market cycle; however, it will be to varying degrees of intensity. The intensity with which one experiences these emotions is a function of what originally motivated the individual to participate in the marketplace.

Individuals who are motivated by conserving capital will maintain a huge advantage over those who are primarily concerned with creating newfound wealth. The former group will be focused on profit-taking and hedging while the latter will be overwhelmed with euphoria and complacency during the moments of truth.

The emotions outlined in "The Wall Street Cheat Sheet" go a very long way in helping us to understand the collective market psychology at different phases of a hyperwave;

however, it does not tell the whole story. The psychology behind the decision-making process is incredibly nuanced, and there are many more factors at play than we could hope to quantify.

There are usually strong social factors at play, such as a deep desire to improve one's lifestyle or social status. Humans also have an innate desire to be right that is combined with a terror of being wrong. Some choose to stay out of the market for reasons that have nothing to do with ambitions of profit or fear of losing. The social stigma of investing in a tobacco or marijuana company will outweigh the soundness of the investment for most people.

There are countless opportunities to profit from investments. The question remains is this: why is an individual looking at this one asset specifically? More often than not it will be a tip from a friend, family member, or financial advisor.

"XYZ just beat their earnings report by 40%! Their stock is up 2% since that news came out, and it was already one of the best-performing assets since the invention of the internet. Now is the time to buy big!"

After getting a tip along those lines, it is up to an individual to make a decision. Many will choose to blindly trust that person's advice and perform minimal due diligence of his or her own. When the person takes responsibility for his or her actions is when the fun of the decision-making process begins.

The Keynesian Beauty Contest goes a long way to help us understand the underlying motivation that one may have for choosing to invest. This was a theoretical contest that asked individuals to identify the six most attractive faces out of a group of one hundred photographs.

> "It is not a case of choosing those [faces] that, to the best of one's judgment, are really the prettiest, nor even those that average opinion genuinely thinks the prettiest. We have reached the third degree where we devote our intelligence to anticipating what average opinion expects the average opinion to be.[13]"

---

[13] Keynes, John Maynard (1936). *The General Theory of Employment, Interest and Money*. New York: Harcourt Brace and Co.

When buying a stock or commodity, it may not be necessarily prudent to choose the one that you think is most destined for success. Instead, it would be a better strategy to pick the asset that you believe is most desirable to the crowd of investors. By extension, it would be an even better strategy to try to anticipate what everyone else thinks everyone else thinks are the soundest investments.

In the end, it is like a big game of rock paper scissors where the two participants are teammates instead of competitors. In this game of rock, paper, scissors it is only possible to win by both using the same method of attack, and it requires no prior collaboration. If we both throw rock, we win. If we throw something different, we both lose. There is only one chance to win.

In that game, I am thinking about what you are going to choose while you are thinking about what I am going to choose. This would be an accurate representation of how many individuals decide to buy, sell, or hold.

"Everyone else seems to be buying, and I don't want to get left out."

"I am not selling here because the whales are going to pump the price."

"XYZ was just on the news beating another earnings report. Everyone else is going to be rushing to buy, so I should get in asap! Heck, I should have listened to my friend and bought last quarter!"

"Person B told me to buy, and he is a financial advisor; therefore, I bet there are a lot of other financial advisors telling people to buy."

Making a decision is the first part of the conditioning process. Profits cultivate positive reinforcement, and negative reinforcement comes from losses. When one takes responsibility for one's decisions, then that person can learn from mistakes and evolve. However, when an individual places the blame on outside sources, such as receiving bad advice, then it is impossible to improve. Therefore, the most important part about the decision-making process is taking responsibility.

Deciding to Hold

Now that one has entered, the decision becomes a question of whether or not to hold or exit. The emotions relating to each decision will be defined by how the asset performed following the initial decision to enter.

In Profit

While in profit, many will not be thinking about selling. Instead, they will be thinking about how to increase exposure.

"I invested X three months ago, and look at how much I am up! I sure wish I would have invested 2X or even 3X!"

This group of people will be focused on all the wrong decisions, such as how to raise cash to increase exposure. This person is consumed with thoughts of selling other investments, working more hours, selling personal belongings, and using or increasing leverage.

This person is not making a rational decision to hold. Instead, he or she is starting to feel the effects of greed. Instead of being happy with their good investment, they are feeling anxious and hopeful that this will be the one thing that allows them to achieve a means to an end.

Adding onto a position that is moving in one's favor comes at the expense of increasing the average cost basis. This is another way that people get trapped at or near the top. When they should have been capitalizing on the profit, they were increasing their risk.

This lies in stark contrast to a person who is primarily concerned with preserving capital as opposed to creating it. The former is likely to start taking profit as soon as the position begins moving in his or her favor to decrease cost basis and minimize risk. The latter is inclined to do exactly the opposite.

By trimming the position, smart money can guarantee a break-even trade or even a small profit. After that person gets further in the profit, then they might continue to hedge through buying puts or taking more off the table. This person might feel a tinge of greed and wished that he or she invested more; however, that will not overwhelm their thought process or control their decision making.

Underwater

The emotions felt when a position moves against the entry price will vary widely and are largely a function of preparation, experience, and discipline.

This is not a comfortable feeling for individuals motivated by conserving wealth, and it isn't much more comfortable for individuals trying to create wealth. The latter group will likely have less to lose and therefore will not be as emotionally invested. Nevertheless, emotional attachment is still very likely to control decision-making.

Being mentally prepared for an outcome is likely as important as the reason for assuming the risk in the first place.

Someone with experience will plan for all possible outcomes and have a plan for each. An example follows:

Have X to enter. Starting with 1/3 X. If position moves 5% against then exit and take a loss. If it moves 5% in favor then add another 1/3 of X. If the position moves another 5% in favor then enter the final portion and trail with a 10% stop loss.

Having a game plan greatly removes the emotions and anxiety from the decision-making process. A person without a sound plan will inevitably fall victim to a few common mistakes, such as holding onto a position for too long while it moves in the wrong direction and overexposing when a position moves in favor. The only way to avoid these pitfalls is to execute a consistent and reliable game plan.

Deciding to Sell

As is the case with deciding to hold, the emotions relating to this thought process are generally determined by unrealized profit or loss.

In Profit

Taking profit seems almost impossible for the person who is primarily focused on creating wealth. That person likely has a deep desire for financial freedom, and it is easy to conclude that this is his or her golden ticket, especially if in phase 4 of a hyperwave.

They look at how much profit they have on paper compared to how long it took to achieve and then extrapolate that into the future.

This person is still thinking about adding more and holding indefinitely. Thoughts of taking profit are quickly squelched due to the logic of "If I would have sold at any point throughout the previous months [years], then I would have been wrong and would have missed out on the entire move that followed!"

The person who is primarily concerned with conserving wealth will become uncomfortable experiencing a phase with such unsustainable returns. This is due to an understanding that what goes up will come down and the best way to protect from the downside is to take profit while it is available.

It is often the case that the most responsible individuals will miss out on the biggest legs up, in many cases exiting in phase 3 right when it is the best time to buy. That is okay though because their goals have been achieved and they are not going to risk compromising their discipline or game plan for a few extra bucks.

"I made a fortune getting out too soon," said J. P. Morgan.

The guidelines of hyperwave will never get one out too soon; however, the point remains that taking profit too soon is far superior to holding for too long.

At a Loss

The psychology behind this decision will be primarily defined by exposure, conviction, and experience.

By far the most important factor when it comes to deciding to take a loss is the amount of exposure and therefore the amount of loss that would capitalize on. If an investor just took a small position to test out the waters, then he or she will not have much difficulty when it comes time to exit at a loss.

On the other hand, if that person was overly convinced in the position, then he or she will be at risk of overexposing as price becomes more and more favorable. Those people will likely find themselves overexposed when it comes time to capitalize on the loss. If the loss is more than originally expected or intended, then that person will be inclined to let the trade ride longer than it should in hopes that he or she will be able to exit closer to break even or even slightly in the green.

An individual's decision to overexpose is often a function of how convicted they are in their analysis. If a person becomes absolutely convinced that this thing will be like buying Apple in the 1990s, then they will be much more inclined to overexpose when the price moves against while watching the beloved asset become cheaper and cheaper.

A person's level of conviction in an investment will define their willingness and ability to control risk, which will determine their willingness and ability to capitalize on a loss.

A person with experience understands what it is like to be fully convicted about the direction of the market only to be proven entirely wrong. That person has likely learned from the mistakes of becoming overexposed and failing to properly manage risk, or they have likely given up on trading / investing entirely.

After experiencing enough of those situations, one will realize that controlling risk and effectively managing stop losses is a prerequisite to success. The key is emotional control. Consistently beating the markets requires a sound game plan, and it also requires psychological calcification.

PHASE 2

PHASES OF A HYPERWAVE

CHAPTER 6

FRUSTRATION AND DISINTEREST

Every phase has a unique emotion that is inexplicably linked to each dimension. Phase 1 could best be defined as frustration, boredom, or complete disinterest.

One either does not care or is completely frustrated by the fact that nobody else seems to care. All of the fundamentals could be pointing toward a huge potential upside, yet all the technical evidence suggests that is not going to happen.

Phase 1 is defined by prolonged consolidation that occurs below a horizontal trend line. There should be many attempts to break through resistance without a weekly close above. Once a weekly candle does close above the trend line, then phase 1 is broken and phase 2 is expected to begin.

Keep in mind that it does not always happen as expected. There will be times when a weekly candle closes above phase 1 and then it quickly retraces back to the middle of the trading range. This is considered a bull trap. There will also be times when the price stays above phase 1 and fails to establish phase 2.

An asset is not in a hyperwave until it enters the third phase, so it is important to be careful in the earlier stages.

Bitcoin Phase 1

Let's use Bitcoin as an example. It started developing a hyperwave in 2014 when a long period of consolidation formed phase 1. This followed the 2013–2014 run-up to $1,000 and the crash back to $210 that followed.

Through this frustration, phase 1 distinguishes the true believers from the followers, speculators, and those who were mostly interested in getting rich quick. Holding through the prolonged bear market would require tremendous belief in the underlying fundamentals. Buying in during / after a prolonged bear market would require even more conviction.

Most individuals who make it through a bear market feel as though they are onto something that few others could even begin to comprehend. This feeling of superiority can allow individuals to shirk off the naysayers and pooh-poohers, but it will be very difficult to do that forever. Eventually, individuals will begin to question the soundness of their investment, either through introspection or nagging friends and family.

After two years of going sideways, some will decide they have had enough and will proceed to sell the bottom. Others will decide that it is worth the risk to continue holding indefinitely, but they will lose interest and quit paying attention to the price action or fundamental development. Very few will continue participating in a similar capacity as they did during the bull market phases.

Phase 2 will not be ready to develop until the hope and interest have been drained from the market. Those feelings will then be replaced with uncertainty, frustration, and doubt. These percolating emotions build up pressure within the system. The longer phase 1 stays intact, the more pressure it will build. Every market participant contributes to this pressure through his or her emotional duress.

The pressure can be thought of as a function of these emotions, and the following move, phases 2–7, is a result of how much pressure is built up within the system. In simpler terms, the more emotions that go into phase 1, the more explosive the following move will be.

Due to this principle, phase 1 is the single most important phase of a hyperwave.

A breakout of phase 1 does not imply that the underlying asset will enter a hyperwave. At this point in the game, it is still extremely rare. Assets range all the time, and hyperwaves are very rare. Therefore, very few phase 1's trading ranges will become a hyperwave.

Even though there is a minimal chance of a hyperwave developing, at this point in the game, it still can be a great trading opportunity. Buying on a breakthrough of horizontal resistance is a high probability entry, but that is based on classical charting principles and has little to nothing to do with hyperwave theory.

First entry is triggered when the horizontal resistance of phase 1 is broken.

Very few of these entries will turn into a complete hyperwave. Nevertheless, if an entry is executed and the market proceeds according to the rules of hyperwave, then this position can be held onto all the way through phase 4. That is possible and valid; however, it is extremely rare.

Even when a hyperwave does not form after price breaks through phase 1 there is still a relatively high probability that this will be a profitable entry. There are many ways that a bull market can develop after breaking through horizontal resistance, hyperwave being one of the least common.

Phase 2 is drawn in by connecting the breakout point with the low of the first major correction.

CHAPTER 7

DOUBT

Phase 2 is the least emotional of all phases. It will be a linear move that is at an angle of forty-five degrees or less. The large majority of phase 2's will occur at an angle of thirty to forty-five degrees, which is a very reasonable rate for a market to progress.

This is a linear move that occurs before the market starts to progress in a parabolic manner. Two steps forward, one step back. When the price is first breaking out of phase 1 and entering phase 2, the overwhelming market emotion will be disbelief.

Individuals who have been actively watching the price in phase 1 will have a mentality that is starting to resemble that of Pavlov's dog. The shock, pain, and dissonance that were experienced on each of the prior run-ups toward horizontal resistance will repeatedly test the thresholds of market participants after it fails to realize higher prices.

The majority of the market must become void of hope and overwhelmed with doubt or confusion before phase 1 has done its job. This despair provides the catalyst necessary to break though the extended trading range and enter the second phase.

A trading range represents equilibrium between the sellers and buyers. At the top of the range, the selling pressure is roughly equivalent to the buying pressure at the bottom of the range. Each time the price approaches resistance, the bulls will expect a breakthrough. When that doesn't happen, then the buyers are conditioned through negative reinforcement.

Individuals who cannot cope with the pain any longer will start selling at prices where the demand exceeds supply. If price can support this selling pressure at or near the bottom of a range then it opens the window for price to breakthrough the top.

After this happens, the majority will remain in disbelief. They have been conditioned by the market and the positive stimuli are no longer enough to provoke salivation.

Furthermore, they will feel like their experience has made them wiser when in reality the opposite is usually the case. What is crucial to understand is that groupthink is starting to take over. The majority will be experiencing the same emotions, and those emotions will begin to control thoughts, which will eventually color perception.

The market will ensure that the majority are thinking and feeling a certain way. That is when it has a perpetual habit of doing exactly the opposite of what the group expects.

"Bull trap!"
"Sucker's rally!"

Most are "too smart" to fall for it this time because they have already been fooled once, twice, three times — or more. To the surprise of most, the rally continues and hope will start to seep its way back into the group's thought process.

"Higher highs and lower lows …"
"Check out this bull trend line …"

Slowly but surely, the sentiment will start to change from *disgust to trust.*

Phase 2 is mostly defined by the group regaining hope. Once that turns into trust, then the market is primed to enter phase 3. A phase 2 trend line is drawn by connecting phase 1 to the first *major correction* in phase 2.

A major correction is a subjective term, and often this line will need to be redrawn after getting penciled in. Keep in mind that if a correction pulls back to phase 1, then it cannot be used to draw phase 2. This is a simple retest to see if prior resistance will become support. The major correction must create a higher low above the phase 1 trend line.

Bitcoin Phase 2

It is very important to understand that phase 2 does not constitute a hyperwave. Only 20 percent of phase 2's become a hyperwave. The amount of times that the phase 2 trend line will need to get adjusted, combined with the low chance of it ever becoming a hyperwave, is why this phase has the smallest consequence out of any. We do not believe that is a coincidence when considering this is the least emotional of all phases.

Once the majority of market participants have gained enough trust, it will cause demand to significantly outweigh supply. This change in market sentiment could create an inflection point. Instead of returning to the phase 2 trend line, where most are waiting to buy, it will gain support above that area, and that creates the vertex where phase 3 will begin.

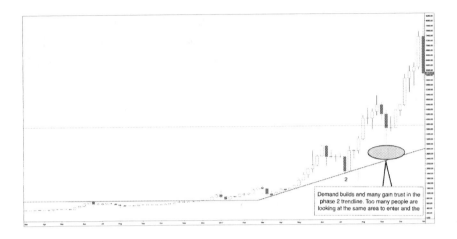

Bitcoin Phase 2 Inflection Point

CHAPTER 8

TRUST

When the market creates a higher low without returning to the phase 2 trend line, then the lowest close should create phase 3.

When drawing phase lines, the most important factor to consider is making sure that there is not one weekly candle that closes below the boundary.

Phase 1 was broken as soon as a weekly candle closed above, and phases 2–4 are broken as soon as a weekly candle closes below. Sometimes the line will need to get adjusted after getting violated, but this should be kept to a minimum.

The next most important factors for drawing correct phase lines are the angles that the trend line creates in relation to the x-axis as well as the vertices coming together at an apex. Each phase will progress at a specific angle, and it is important to confirm that phase lines conform to these parameters. Phase 3 should progress at a forty-five to sixty-degree angle.

Another very important consideration is the vertices between each phase. When phase 3 starts immediately after price tests phase 2, then that would create a perfect apex. The archetype has perfect apexes between each phase and this is ideal, although extremely rare.

The last factor to consider is the number of touch points that the phase line has. If a phase line meets all the guidelines above but only has two touch points, then it is very suspect. The more touch points that a trend line has, the stronger it becomes.

Using the parameters above, let's examine the two charts below to see which phase line is preferable.

1

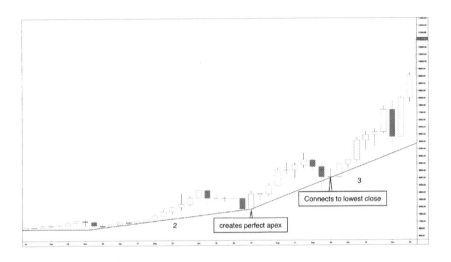

Bitcoin Phase 3 with Apex

2

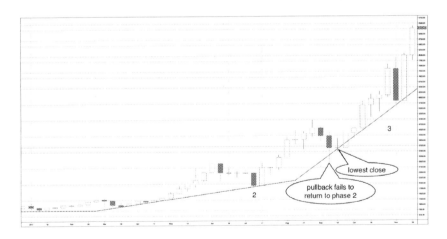

Bitcoin Phase 3 with More Touch Points

The pullback in September 2017 found support before retesting the phase 2 line. This tells us that we should start penciling in a new phase 3 trend line that connects phase 2 to the lowest close from the pullback.

Both trend lines above create a nice angle that is well within reason for a phase 3. Both also have all weekly candles closing above the trendlines. Chart 1 sees the phase lines creating a perfect apex, while chart 2 does not create an ideal apex but does have more touch points.

Both phase lines abide by the most important rules; therefore, both could be considered valid. However, we want to assess which one is best. The phase 3 line in chart 1 is preferable because vertices are more important than touch points.

After phase 3 is established, then we can consider the asset to be in a hyperwave. Approximately 85 percent of phase 3's complete the pattern, while the other 15 percent of snowflakes are not in the right environment to crystalize. Think of the 15 percent as raindrops that started as snowflakes. The conditions in the cumulonimbus were sufficient to create snowflakes, but the temperature below was not able to sustain them.

As traders, we are glorified gamblers who understand that nothing is a sure thing. However, 85 percent is more than enough of an imbalance to start betting on the outcome. This is when the emotions are starting to ramp up, and it represents the best opportunity to build long exposure.

Trust is turning into lust.

Confidence gradually increases as the price continues to rally. The increased angle of the phase line means that there is more velocity, which is another way of saying that there will be a greater return on investment in a shorter amount of time. This will reinforce the confidence that is starting to control the group's thought processes.

Instead of getting chastised by family and friends, the market participants will start to field probing questions.

"So what is the deal with Bitcoin? I just saw on CNN that it is up more than 100 percent in less than two months ..."

"I wish I would have bought a couple of months ago. Do you think it is too late to buy now?"

This will further reinforce the confidence that the group is feeling. Individuals who did enter two months ago, or earlier, will feel like they are on the inside while the outsiders start to feel afraid of getting left out in the cold.

Phase 3 is by far the best time to enter. The group will mostly think that the train has already left the station and that the best time to buy was yesterday, last week, last month, or last year. Yet again, the majority is wrong. Even if buying earlier would provide a better cost basis, the fact remains that the risk-reward and strike rate will never be better than entering in phase 3.

Professionals focus on risk versus reward, while the group thinks about buying in at the cheapest possible price or making the greatest possible profit.

The best way to trade hyperwaves is buying at or near the phase 3 trend line and selling as soon as a weekly candle closes below phase 4.

As phase 3 progresses, the adoption will continue to spread and market participants will feel more and more emboldened while others feel more and more on the outside. The longer this reinforcement loop continues, the greater the chances of establishing a fourth phase.

CHAPTER 9

EUPHORIA

The fourth phase of a hyperwave is when things get very interesting. Emotions run rampant while logic fades into the background. Phase 4 will come with disbelief similar to phase 2. Even the most optimistic early adopters will have a very hard time wrapping their heads around the rapidly increasing valuations.

Most expectations are exceeded in phase 3. The group thought that it was too late to enter during phase 3 and this is the first time they are happy to be proven wrong. Even though the value has far exceeded everyone's wildest dreams, the large majority will not have the wherewithal to take profit.

Instead, most will be thinking along the lines of trying to increase exposure. After watching so many pullbacks rally hard off of support, many will start setting their sights on buying the next dip. This frenzy will cause most to throw caution into the wind. Those who do will become severely overexposed as a result.

Controlling exposure is the last line of defense against the emotions that are becoming overwhelming. Those who fail to embrace this tactic will undoubtedly end up suffering the brunt of the pain that follows.

Another inflection point will occur, and that will give birth to the fourth phase. When everyone starts salivating at buying a correction, then the corrections will likely cease to occur. That will eventually create the fourth and most powerful bull phase.

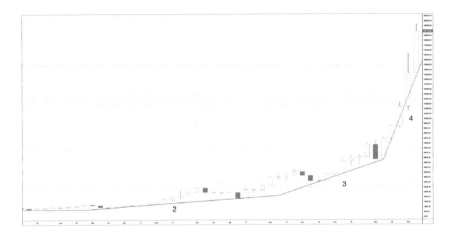

Bitcoin Phase 4

Phase 4 will proceed at an angle of sixty to ninety degrees, which means the price will be leaping forward without glancing back. This will progress until it appears riskier to be on the outside than it is to enter late.

Individuals who thought they were too late in phase 3 will start buying phase 4. Others who saw no value in the product in phases 1, 2, or 3 will start buying phase 4. Ones who kind of understood the value but perceived the risk to outweigh the reward in earlier phases will start buying phase 4.

Previously there were intermittent news stories that piqued the interest of outsiders, and now those stories are almost unavoidable. Multiple news outlets are covering it as well as all the newspapers and magazines. Eventually, it becomes the talk of the town. Those who entered are geniuses for taking the leap of faith; those who did not enter feel left behind and somewhat incompetent for allowing that to happen.

The fear of getting left behind is a deep-seated emotion that likely finds its roots thousands of years ago when we were hunter-gatherers and being ostracized was a severe hindrance on one's ability to survive. If the majority of the tribe is deciding to go one direction, then choosing a different orientation will trigger tremendous angst.

On the one hand, a person deeply desires to have his or her beliefs proven correct, especially when it means others are wrong. On the other hand, the reward of this egotistical satisfaction will pale in comparison to the risk of being unable to survive.

Outsiders sense that something is amiss when the market participants are overwhelmed with euphoria. Strong-minded individuals who stick to their morals during times of duress will likely be able to listen to their gut and remain on the sidelines. Others will begin to fall in line as the desire to be right is replaced with a fear of missing out, which is known colloquially as FOMO.

The longer those individuals wait, the more it will feel like they are missing out on the next big thing. Inevitably these unfortunate souls will become the high-water mark of the hyperwave pattern.

If phase 3 is defined by confidence, then phase 4 is characterized by hubris and elation of insiders and the overwhelming FOMO of outsiders.

"You would have to be crazy not to own any Bitcoin! It is going to uproot the entire system!"

"No way am I selling. Buying and holding is a must!"

Lust turns into must.

A weekly close below the phase 4 trend line indicates the top of the hyperwave. The markup phase is complete and what follows is the wake. At this point, it is time to count the chicklings and take full profit.

Individuals who do not take profit are being motivated by a combination of arrogance and greed. This will be the prevailing thoughts and feelings of the group. Inevitably pride will precede the fall.

CHAPTER 10

GREED AND DELUSION

An asset enters phase 5 once there is a weekly close below phase 4. When this happens, the fate is sealed and there is an approximately 99 percent chance that the asset will return to phase 1. Very few will be able to wrap their heads around this in real time. That is mainly due to the magnitude of the price discrepancy and the emotional roller coaster that is phase 3 and phase 4.

Even though the large majority will not know it yet, breaking down phase 4 and entering phase 5 is where the

lust turns into a bust.

The fifth phase is the first corrective trend line, out of two total. It will come with the appearance of being the dip that everyone was waiting to buy in phase 4 and/or at the inflection point of phase 3. This will give individuals one more chance to become overexposed. Similar to dropping a line into a barrel full of fish phase 5 will get plenty of bites.

After watching every correction bounce hard and fast off support, the group will become overconfident in this repeating once more. Instead of taking profit, the crowd will be consumed with the idea of increasing exposure before the next big wave to the upside.

Greed is rarely rewarded by the marketplace, and this is a perfect example. The asset has already exceeded the herd's wildest expectations, but instead of feasting on profits from the cash cow, they line up for a one-way trip to the slaughterhouse. The group follows this path as a result of delusion and refusing to read the writing on the wall.

CHAPTER 11

COMPLACENCY AND
SELF-SATISFACTION

Phase 6 is analogous to a cat's tenth life. It will come with the appearance of landing on its feet while providing the strong bounce that everyone was expecting. This will further reinforce the herd's conviction that the market is in for another big move to the upside. Unfortunately, it will not be the golden goose everyone is banking on. Instead, it will simply be the first dead cat bounce, of which there will be many to follow.

The overwhelming emotion in phase 6 is complacency. Individuals who were arrogant become smug and self-satisfied while watching this bounce approach all-time highs. To most, another big move to the upside is more of a question of when not if.

Greed is rarely rewarded, and hubris is always properly punished. The jig is up when phase 6 creates a lower high below phase 4's all-time high. The greedy individuals who are focused on increasing exposure, instead of taking profit, will be hurt the worst. A close second will be the egotistical individuals who have their world turned completely upside down in a matter of weeks, days, or sometimes hours.

Another bust bites the dust.

We have often wondered why hyperwaves still exist. Not only do they continue to prevail in every type of market, but their prominence and frequency are waxing instead of waning. This pattern repeats itself over and over again without significant variations.

Why haven't we learned from our mistakes? Why hasn't this pattern evolved or mutated in some fashion?

The only explanation is the underlying emotions that continue to repeat themselves at each step of the way. As long as market participants continue to be blinded by emotion, then it will be nearly impossible for them to learn from the consequences. Most will fall into two categories.

- giving up on actively watching/trading the markets and either staying away entirely or submitting to a buy-and-hold strategy
- simply taking some time off to recover psychologically and then inevitably continuing to make the same mistakes after returning

CHAPTER 12

GRIEF

Heard the singers playin', How we cheered for more,
The crowd then rushed together, Tryin' to keep warm,
Still the rain kept pourin', Fallin' on my ears,
And I wonder, still I wonder,
Who'll stop the rain?

—John Fogarty

Phase 7 is the most maniacal of all phases. It is the slaughterhouse that the group was being prodded toward during phases 5 and 6. This is when the music stops playing and everyone suddenly realizes that there is nowhere to sit.

Phase 7 is different from all other phases in that it will continue to break through the trend line with a weekly close above it. If any of the other phases are violated on a weekly closing basis, then it means the phase is invalidated. In phase 7, this will happen over and over again. No matter how many times this happens, the phase remains intact.

There is only one thing that can invalidate a phase 7 once it has begun, and that is a close above phase 4's all-time high. About one out of five hyperwaves will find support from phase 3 or phase 2 and then go on to create a new all-time high. These are considered funky hyperwaves, and we will cover these unique patterns later in this book. The other 80 percent of hyperwaves that enter phase 7 are all aboard a train that is making a roundtrip from phase 1.

General Electric is a great example of just how maniacal phase 7 can be while remaining intact. The first chart shows how a new phase 7 trend line is drawn after the prior one gets violated. Phase 7 should start at the top of phase 6, and it should get continually adjusted every time a weekly candle closes above. The second chart shows how phase 7 is currently drawn.

General Electric Phase 7 Adjustments

General Electric Hyperwave

This is a good example of why one should be rooting for a return to phase 1 if one eventually wants a new all-time high. If it gets close and makes a strong bounce before reaching its destination, then that only prolongs the process—sometimes by decades.

A dead cat bounce that lasts for more than eight years will be very difficult to identify as such, unless one fully understands and believes in hyperwave theory.

More Examples of Maniacal Phase 7's

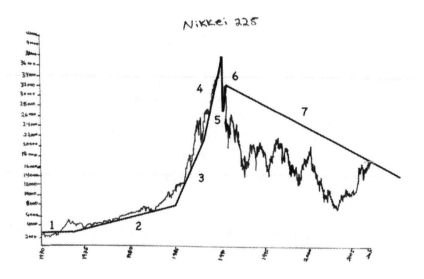

**Nikkei 225 (NI225) Hyperwave Broke through Phase 7
Multiple Times before Continuing Down Trend**

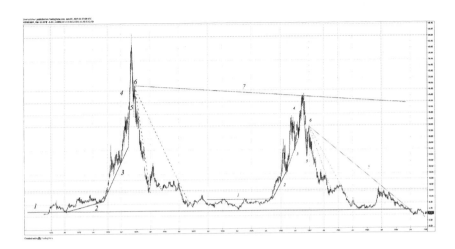

1972–1984 Sugar Hyperwave

Sugar is the most maniacal phase 7 that we have ever seen (until Bitcoin). It formed a hyperwave fractal (see page 88) while in phase 7. We had never seen anything like this before (until Bitcoin). There are a couple more reasons why this chart is extremely intriguing.

Notice how close the price came to returning to phase 1 in July 1978 before eventually going on the second run-up.

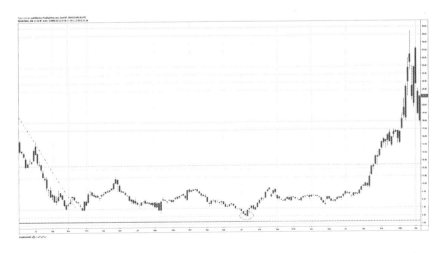

Closeup of Sugar in July 1978

Phase 1 waited at $5.64, and the price closed at $6.13 on July 17, 1978. That is only 7.99 percent away after a 90 percent decrease. If it would have returned to phase 1, then the hyperwave would have been over. Instead, the phase 1 target remained intact as did the hyperwave pattern as long as price remained below the prior all-time high of $65.

The next intriguing aspect of this chart is how the peak of the second bubble topped below the high of phase 6. Once phase 6 is established, it is formidable resistance and we do not expect it to get violated during phase 7.

Sugar rallied 729 percent after the low on July 17, 1978, but it stopped just shy of phase 6's peak before entering a fierce fifth phase. Yet again the price comes within a whisker of returning to phase 1, and instead of completing the pattern, it went on another, much smaller, parabolic move that saw the price increase 100 percent in eleven weeks.

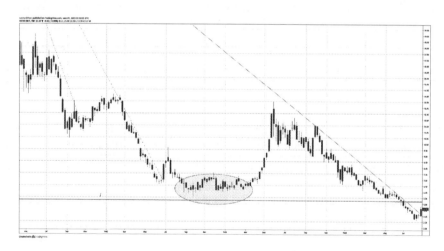

Sugar Nearly Returns to Phase 1 in the Winter of 1982–1983

On the last week of June 1982, the price finally fell below phase 1, but it didn't close below. Returning to phase 1 requires a close below the horizontal trend line. The following week, the price did close below phase 1, which finally completed the pattern.

This shows how powerful phase 7 is. The final phase of a hyperwave provides an overwhelming amount of downward pressure until the pattern completes.

Maniacal is almost certainly an understatement. Very few fall straight to the target, and the overwhelming majority eventually get there. It is often said that the market's purpose is to separate the most amount of people from the most amount of money, and phase 7 is the epitome of this concept.

Losing actual money and/or watching life-changing profits slip through one's fingertips leads to an enormous amount of consternation, panic, desperation, and depression. These emotions almost always lead to very poor decision-making, which is the hallmark of the maddening final phase.

The seventh phase is defined by a variety of emotions that seem very in line with Kübler-Ross' model of the seven stages of grief[14][15].

The Kübler-Ross model[16] was developed to express the different emotional states that one grapples with after being diagnosed as terminally ill. The seven stages of grief model was developed to explain the emotional cycle that one experiences as a response to losing a loved one. We find it extremely interesting that a very similar cycle is experienced when the hyperwave enters the terminal seventh phase.

A few emotions can be added to the seven stages, such as anxiety and panic. The final stage of acceptance is not included on this chart because it will come at the tail end of phase 7, generally as it is making the final descent to phase 1.

---

[14] Kübler-Ross, Elisabeth; Kessler, David (2014). *On grief & grieving : finding the meaning of grief through the five stages of loss*. New York: Scribner.

[15] *7 Stages of Grief: A Guide To Morning* (2018, June 4). Retrieved from https://www.thrivetalk.com/7-stages-of-grief/

[16] A diagram developed by Bertrand Grondin from a presentation of Elisabeth Kübler Ross; ideas produced by France Telecom.

Stages of grief

In phase 6, nobody can believe that it would be possible to return to such low prices. Once those prices are discovered, then it will cause the group to finally accept their fate. Yet again it comes at exactly the wrong time. This acceptance will often cause long-term holders to capitulate and sell—often at a loss. Once the market becomes overwhelmed with disgust, the price will find a bottom.

Biting the dust leads to utter disgust.

Unwarranted selling pressure will continue until it reaches prices where the demand far exceeds supply. There will be tremendous selling volume that will challenge or exceed the largest volume spikes the asset has ever experienced. When the record-selling volume finds enough support and fails to push the price down further, then the bottom will be found—at least for the time being.

It is important to understand that some hyperwaves go to the slaughterhouse and are never heard from again. A return to phase 1 means that the hyperwave has completed its round-trip journey. It does not imply that another hyperwave will follow. Once it completes, then it is over and no more predictions can be made based on the theory. All things are possible from that point on, including the following:

- continue selling off and go to $0
- never create a new all-time high but retain a value >$0

- create an all-time high without creating a new hyperwave
- consolidate at that price level for an extended period of time, potentially creating a new phase 1
    - if this occurs, then it is prudent to be on the watch for another hyperwave to form in the future; however, one would still need to wait for a confirmed phase 3 to validate that another hyperwave is taking place
    - still could create a new phase 3 and be one of the 15 percent that breaks down before entering phase 4

What happens after a return to phase 1 is anyone's guess.

PHASE 3

HISTORY OF HYPERWAVES

CHAPTER 13

HISTORICAL HYPERWAVES

Thirty-Year Interest Rates Yield

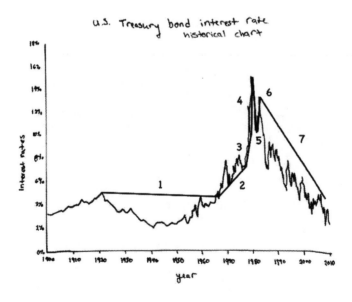

US Bond Interest Rate Hyperwave

This is the biggest hyperwave we have ever found. That doesn't mean it is the largest there ever was. What you will notice, just as with snowflakes, is that no two are the same even though they have almost identical characteristics. The amplitude of phase 4, length of phase 2, angle of phase 3 will always be slightly different but very similar.

Whenever you are looking at a phase 1, you want it to go all the way across the chart so that you can make sure it returns, which it did here. It is always perfectly horizontal. Not only is this the biggest hyperwave we have found, but it is also the most important macroeconomically; we will delve into the implications later in this book.

Below our analysis is limited to monthly charts. Unfortunately, this is all we can find for the hyperwaves that are mostly a century old. If anyone knows where we can find weekly charts, then it would be greatly appreciated.

Allied Chemical and Dyes

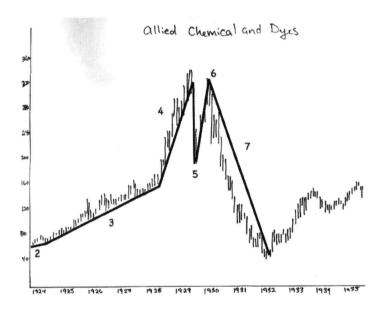

Allied Chemical & Dyes

Phase 1 ran anywhere from 1908–1914 to 1922 on all these charts we are about to examine.

The two terminal points of a hyperwave are a repeating theme that are important to pay close attention to. First occurs when phase 4 is broken. That happens when a weekly candle closes below the phase line, which marks the terminal point of the bull market.

Approximately 80 percent of hyperwaves that enter phase 7 are scheduled to proceed to the second terminal point, which is phase 1. To be one of the 20 percent, the price should find support from the second or third phase line and then proceed to create a new all-time high.

Assets that enter phase 7 and create a new all-time high after finding support from phase 2 or phase 3 are considered funky hyperwaves. These aberrations are still expected to return to the second terminal point; however, they seem to prefer a much more scenic route.

Creating a new all-time high without returning to phase 1 does not imply that the asset is out of the woods; instead, it is likely only delaying the inevitable.

Allied Chemical & Dyes was a traditional hyperwave. It took the more direct route of returning to phase 1 without exceeding the phase 6 peak. After returning to the second terminal point, it just drifted sideways. This is not uncommon.

Allis Chalmers Energy Inc. (ALY)

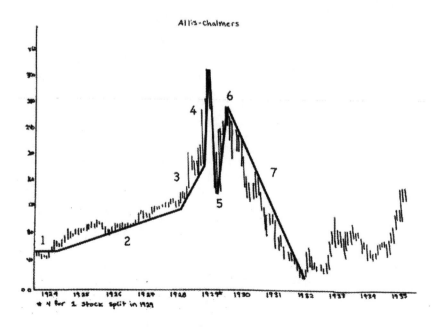

Allis Chalmers Energy Inc. (ALY)

You can see the angles as they are getting higher and higher, then finally the run-up to the top. You want to take quick looks at the amplitude of these.

In this case, we see a run from $10 to $80, which is an 800 percent move. That is on the lower end of what a hyperwave is expected to return. Most are between 800 percent and 2,000 percent.

We will continue to stress the time element. This does not occur over short periods of time. Bubbles can occur over short periods of time, but hyperwaves take time to develop.

The shortest hyperwaves occur in the more volatile and illiquid markets, such as mining shares or cryptocurrency.

We have never seen one occur as quickly as Bitcoin, which has been active for about five years and eleven months at the time of writing. About 60 percent of that time was spent in phase 1, and these proportions are common.

Phase 1 specifically takes a long time to develop, and that is a primary reason why hyperwaves do not occur over short periods of time.

Now look at 1929 to 1960 to examine what happens once a hyperwave gets back to its second terminal point. Notice how Allis Chalmers didn't do a thing for the next twenty-five to thirty years after reaching its second terminal point.

Anaconda Mining Inc.

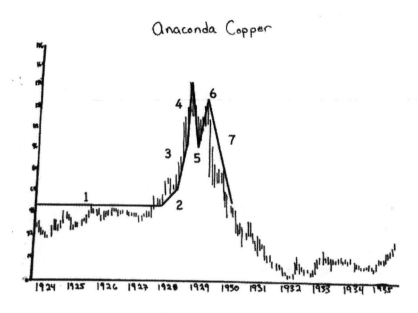

Anaconda Mining Inc. (ANXGF)

You will notice the examples we are using are not specific to one sector or industry. Here we have a very small hyperwave in amplitude, but the duration is the same as the other ones from this time period.

When hyperwaves are abundant, then many assets will follow the leader. The market leaders will tend to have the most impressive gains. The followers will generally form a similar pattern while experiencing smaller returns.

This is a good example of why it is important to understand the macroeconomic shift that is causing hyperwaves to form. The companies and commodities that are most closely associated with the shift are likely to be the market leaders and therefore the best performers.

The hyperwaves that were experienced in the early 1900s were largely a result of the Industrial Revolution. Anaconda was a copper company, and it benefited from this progression; however, it did not perform as well as some other resources, such as petroleum.

Bethlehem Steel

Bethlehem Steel Corp. Stocks (NYSE: BS)

The first phase of a hyperwave needs to have all price action below the horizontal trend line, and it should also have many touch points. The touch points represent price rallying toward resistance and failing to break through. This should happen over and over again before eventually establishing phase 2.

Nevertheless, it is possible to have a double phase 1. This occurs when a breakthrough of the first phase 1 does not lead to a second phase. Instead, the price breaks through horizontal resistance turn that into support and then proceed to go sideways for another prolonged period of time. This means that a new horizontal trend line can be drawn to illustrate the second area of resistance.

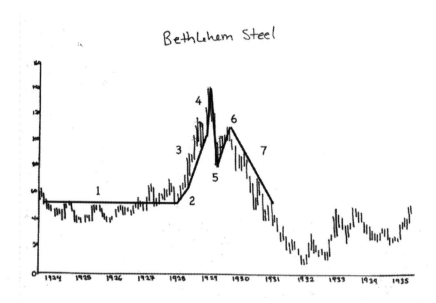

Bethlehem Steel Corp Double Phase 1

Bethlehem Steel is an example of a double phase 1. Nothing happened with steel companies until the very end of the 1950s. Remember that phase 1 is the most important phase of a hyperwave, and the longer it lasts, the more explosive the move should be.

Think of a hyperwave as a volcano. The final eruption is a function of how long the pressure builds. Pressure continues to build while the magma percolates below the surface. Erupting is only a matter of time since there is no other way to release the energy.

Steel companies took longer to establish phase 2 than their counterparts. This means that their phase 1's were longer in duration and therefore contained more pressure. After they finally erupted, the following moves were tremendous.

Correctly identifying phase 1 is also important because that becomes the target after price enters phase 7 and breaks down phase 2. If phase 1 is not properly identified then the corresponding phase 7 target will be askew.

An ideal phase 1 will be easily identifiable and would look similar to the following:

Ideal Phase 1

A perfected phase 1 has a very tight/narrow range with a clear area of resistance that price consistently tests and fails to close above. A tight range that lasts for years provides the greatest amount of pressure for the following move. Phase 1's that are short, occur in wide ranges, or have a double phase 1 are not ideal. It makes the pattern difficult to properly identify, and it suggests that there is less pent-up pressure. The latter implies that the following move would be far less significant.

The Bethlehem Steel hyperwave did not even appreciate 300 percent. Such a small amplitude is likely a result of the very short double phase 1.

Notice what happened to Bethlehem Steel after it returned to phase 1. From the 1930s to the early 1950s, Bethlehem Steel went flat. Hyperwave theory does not make any predictions in regard to what will happen to the price following a return to phase 1; however, this prolonged sideways action is quite common as we are starting to see.

Fiat Chrysler Automobiles NV

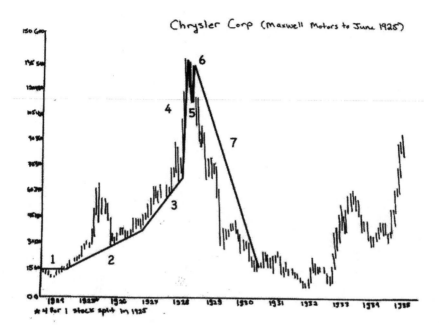

Fiat Chrysler Automobiles NV (NYSE: FCAU)

There was funny stuff going on partly because of the split in 1925. Splits are handled differently today, such that they do not impact the technicals in the same way they might have in the early 1900s. We are not sure how chartists handled splits during the 1920's. Nevertheless, what was interesting is price came right back down to the phase 2 trend line before continuing to move up.

Chrysler does not really have a phase 5 or phase 6 on this chart. We think that would change if it was a weekly chart.

This one began to move fairly quickly from the bottom.

Auto companies did well throughout the 1950s, but we don't see any kind of tremendous move even though the US was building, building, building, and spending, spending, spending.

Perhaps the most interesting part about this chart is the action that occurred shortly after breaking through phase 1 in 1925. The market took off in a parabolic fashion and returned close to 400 percent in one year. When looking closely it appears that this formed a Funky Fractal as the phase 7 breakdown found support from phase 2 and went on to create a new all time high.

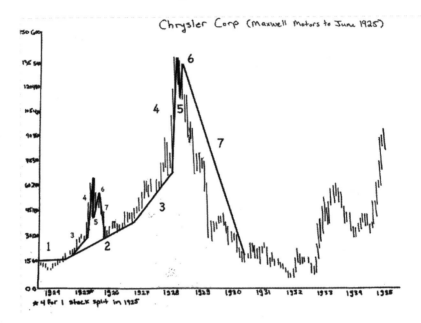

DuPont de Nemours, Inc. (NYSE: DD) (Formerly the Dow Chemical Company)

When looking at the next chart, Dow Chemical, notice how similar the two appear. Strong corollaries can also be drawn with the Nasdaq 100 and McDonald's funky hyperwaves, both of which are included in this book.

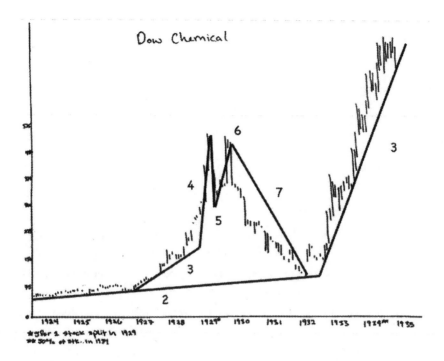

DuPont de Nemours, Inc. (NYSE: DD) (Formerly the Dow Chemical Company)

Phase 6 came very close to taking out the all-time high created in phase 4, but it did not do it. This also looks like a funky hyperwave, finding support from phase 2 and going on to create a new all-time high. This is the earliest example of such an occurrence that we have found. Hyperwaves are very rare, and funky hyperwaves are even more unique. This is the oldest one we have found, but that doesn't mean it is the oldest one that exists. There are almost certainly older examples that we have yet to come across.

We like the fact that there is no new phase 1. If this is a funky hyperwave, there should not be a new phase 1 because all the price action should remain above the angular phase 2 before establishing a new 3.

To test that theory, we would need a weekly chart. The monthly chart makes it appear as though all the price action is above phase 2, but that would need to be confirmed with weekly closes. If it qualifies, then it is an enormous funky hyperwave we need to explore more. As it stands, this looks like the longest hyperwave that has ever occurred.

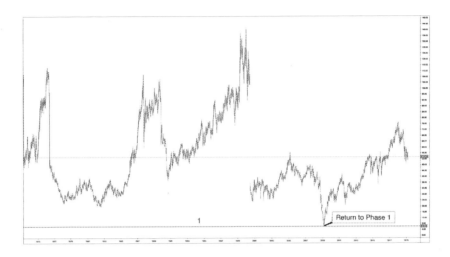

Dow Chemicals, Now Known as DowDupont, Returns to Phase 1 in 2009

Phase 1 was waiting at around $6, but the phase 2 trend line proved to be too resilient to allow for a return to that area, at least for the time being. Over the next eighty years, the price rallied to over $100 and looked as though it was going to leave the century-old phase 1 in the rearview mirror for good.

That all changed at the turn of the millennium. From 1999 to 2008, the price fell from $141 to $6.10. Even though it took more than one hundred years, this funky hyperwave finally reached its second terminal point.

This provides strong evidence that even funky hyperwaves are unable to avoid their destiny. Taking the scenic route could delay this much longer than is imaginable while experiencing massive returns in the meantime. However, as long as the pattern is active, revisiting the second terminal point is to be expected.

General Electric

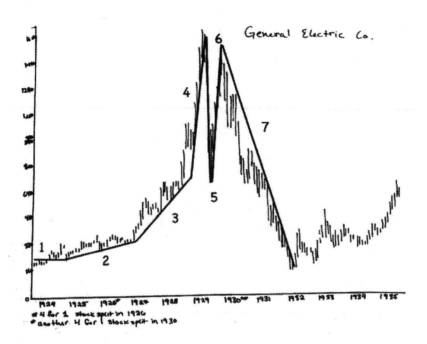

General Electric Company (NYSE: GE)

The General Electric hyperwave during the early 1900s is the best real-world example that we have found. Remember that the closer the pattern is to the archetype, the more likely it is to abide by the rules. When the rules are this reliable, and the patterns are this prevalent, it is very important to look for the best examples and shy away from any that display significant deformities.

This is the blue-ribbon winner that other candidates should be compared to. The archetype is a perfect illustration in an imperfect world and this is the best real world example that we have found.

We are fascinated by this one for a variety of reasons. Not only because of the chart above but also due to what happened afterward. From 1936 to the 1960s, it did not make it back up to its peak. From 1970 to 1983, it went sideways. This created a new phase 1, and sure enough, another hyperwave followed.

The second hyperwave is not nearly as perfected, but it certainly fits the bill. What is so interesting about the second GE hyperwave is phase 7. It has lasted from 2001 to present and has been one of the wildest phase 7's that we have ever seen.

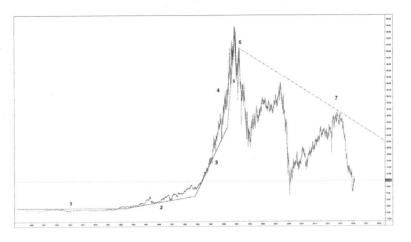

Second Hyperwave in General Electric

ITT Inc.

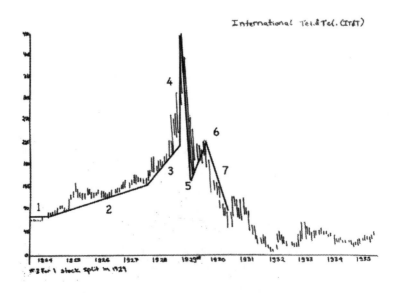

ITT Inc. (NYSE: ITT)

Phase 5 depreciated close to 150 percent from phase 4's all-time high. That is unusually large for the fifth phase. It retraced more than the entire phase 4 move. Phase 6 is also quite abnormal.

We expect to see a strong dead cat bounce that works its way toward prior all-time highs and traps in the bulls who have grown accustomed to buying the dip. In this case, the price simply consolidated in a sideways manner instead of bouncing. This is important to note for individuals who prefer to exit during phase 6.

Often a trader or investor can get a better price on his or her exit by waiting to sell phase 6 instead of selling the first weekly close phase 4, as the rules suggest. This is a valid approach; however, it is important to keep in mind that not all phase 6's provide a bounce. In rare situations the price will simply consolidate sideways before breaking down into phase 7. Such was the case with IT&T, and it was combined with an abnormally large phase 5 that almost wiped out all the proceeds from phases 3 and 4 combined.

After dropping from $150 to $5, it just went sideways for years. Thirty years later, in 1960, it still had not gotten back to the all-time high.

1953 and 1954 are when most of the others returned to their peak and the Dow Jones Industrials made a new all-time high. It is interesting to consider why IT&T lagged so far behind.

CHAPTER 14

HOW TYLER FIRST DISCOVERED HYPERWAVE

In 1980 Tyler was looking at two charts while on the phone with a high net worth client. He proceeded to describe the sugar chart while unknowingly looking at silver. He didn't realize his mistake until after hanging up the telephone. They were so identical that Tyler started to wonder what could have led to two very dissimilar commodities forming very similar patterns. After looking at a few more charts, he drew the hyperwave archetype, and it has remained unchanged ever since.

Shortly thereafter, Tyler started looking into a lot of commodities, and it turned out to be the best time to get into them. The 1970s was a very unusual period for commodities, mainly due to Nixon closing the gold window.

Under the Bretton Woods system, which was established in July 1944, the US dollar was the reserve currency for the rest of the world. Foreign currencies were backed by US dollars, which were convertible to gold based on fixed exchange rates.

In the 1960s, the United States ran its first non-war deficit under President John F. Kennedy. The world rebelled against inflation because the US dollar no longer provided the security that it was meant to under the Bretton Woods system, and it soon began losing value relative to foreign currencies.

This caused a run on the bank of the US dollar at a scale the world had never experienced. Entire countries moved to exchange their US dollar reserves for physical gold. France was the most aggressive seller of greenbacks and sent a warship to New York in 1971 to collect the remainder of its gold. Eventually the vaults were effectively emptied, and the jig was up.

On August 15, 1971, the United States defaulted on its obligation to convert US dollars to gold. This closed the gold window that was opened under Bretton Woods, which removed the last linkage of government money to the scarce commodity. This thrust the world into the current fiat[17] currency based monetary system that we are still beholden to.

The country then entered a very high-interest-rate/high-inflationary period, and many commodities took off as a result, including but not limited to gold, silver, cocoa, sugar, and oil.

The Organization of the Petroleum Exporting Countries (OPEC) came together and held the world hostage to how much oil it would sell. Oil boomed, and this further exacerbated inflation. It wasn't only that. Countries began to print money in an unprecedented fashion.

The United States led the way in money printing, starting in 1961 and 1962 under John F. Kennedy. For the first time in US history, the Fed ran a deficit without a war to fund.

The rest of the world followed suit shortly thereafter, and by 1980, things really started to get out of hand.

---

[17] Fiat money is government-issued currency declared as legal tender and its value is backed by the government that has issued it

In 1979 Paul Volker was named the president of the Federal Reserve, and he made it his mission to kill inflation. To accomplish this goal, he raised the Fed funds rate to levels that were previously unheard of.[18]

An inversion of the yield curve happens when short-term interest rates are greater than long-term interest rates. This is highly indicative of the top of a bull market and/or the beginning of a bear market.

Banks borrow from the Federal Reserve at the short-term interest rates and will lend at the long-term rates. The difference between the two represents the banks' profit or net interest margin. Short-term rates exceeding long-term rates implies that banks would be lending at a loss. As a result, they will quit loaning, and this will cause liquidity to evaporate.

When Volker forced the Fed funds rate above the ten-year Treasury bonds it inverted the yield curve and caused the economic machine to grind to a halt. This is the primary tactic that the Federal Reserve uses to combat hyperinflation that is a result of irresponsible money printing and lending. This is a very effective strategy in the short term but does little to shore up inflation in the long run. Eventually the rates will need to be normalized, which paves the way for another inflationary cycle.

It is important to note that period in time was extremely unusual, and it happened to serve as the perfect breeding ground for hyperwaves. Closing the gold window, and the excessive money printing that followed was the macroeconomic shift that caused the bubbles that the economy is still experiencing to this day. The short-term defensive tactics have only led to larger and larger bubbles with each inflationary cycle.

Closing the gold window was the first domino to fall, and it directly caused bubbles in commodities as well as interest rates. After interest rates peaked in 1982, the equity markets entered massive bubbles of their own. Decades of declining interest rates led to

---

[18] Gavin and Cook created a great chart published using data from the Federal Reserve Board and the U.S. Treasury depicting the relationship between the Fed Funds Rate and the 10-year Treasury Bond Yield: Gavin, W. T., & Cooke, D. A. (2017, November 24). Ups and Downs of Inflation and Role of Fed Credibility: St. Louis Fed. Retrieved from https://www.stlouisfed.org/publications/regional-economist/april-2014/the-ups-and-downs-of-inflation-and-the-role-of-fed-credibility

the unprecedented inflation that Paul Volker was trying to mitigate. His plan backfired and it was likely because he failed to grasp the long-term repercussions.

Under Paul Volker, interest rates were pushed to artificially high levels. When this occurs in the financial markets, an equal and opposite reaction is expected. The artificially low interest rates that we have experienced since 2008 are just that.

Falling interest rates, with a normalized yield curve, create a risk-on environment for banks who will strive to maximize returns despite consistently dwindling yields. Instead of lending to creditworthy customers, they will prefer subprime applicants because those individuals pay a higher than average interest rate. This is what caused the 2008 mortgage crisis, which was the most recent domino to fall as a result of the policies put into place in the 1970s.

Unfortunately, there are still dominos left standing. We are inclined to think that the final domino will topple when the US indices breakdown the massive hyperwaves that started escalating in 1982. The Dow Jones and S&P 500 are currently in phase 3. Over the past thirty-seven years, they have returned 2,596 percent and 2,690 percent respectively. This is without entering the fourth and most lucrative phase. There is no telling how high these indices will go before the bubble pops.

The current hyperwaves are an indirect result of what happened in the 1970s. The most significant driving factors are the full departure from a sound monetary system and the reaction in interest rates that followed.

It is very important for us intellectually to know that the hyperwaves we are seeing today have not changed in any way from the ones that Tyler studied back in the 1970s and 1980s. The pattern is the same, and the underlying fundamentals are eerily similar as well.

In the 1970s, equities were not doing anything. Nobody knew it at the time, but they were forming phase 1 of a hyperwave. From 1965 to 1982, the Dow Industrials could not get above $1,000. That is the perfect phase 1. Since then we have run from $1,000 up to $26,000, and it remains active.

The 1970s had hyperwaves in commodities because of inflation, which was a result of the world decoupling itself from a sound money standard. The further we removed ourselves from this standard, the more hyperwaves we have experienced as a result. When the money supply increases exponentially it will flow into equities and commodities exponentially.

In this case, the money supply is continuing to increase in a hyperwave, and so is the stock market. Commodities have had smaller, intermittent hyperwaves but nothing like what we have seen out of the S&P 500, Nasdaq, and Dow Jones over the past forty years.

There was another period, not too long ago, when a relatively vast number of hyperwaves occurred simultaneously. That happened at the turn of the twentieth century, from 1879 to 1930. Those moves didn't start accelerating into the parabolic third and fourth phases until shortly after the Federal Reserve was created in 1913.

It took winning a world war to rebound from the meltdown that led to the Great Depression.

As was the case before we are not drawing this comparison in order to frighten readers. Our intention is to begin a discourse about the implications of possibly living through the largest macroeconomic shift that has ever occurred. Throughout this book, we will be describing the problem of hyperwaves as well as providing specific trading rules for how to profit when they occur. Toward the end, we will briefly explore some potential solutions to the problems that are specified or implied.

To understand what shifts are occurring directly under our feet, it is crucial to understand the most important hyperwave that has ever occurred: the yield rate of thirty-year US Treasuries.

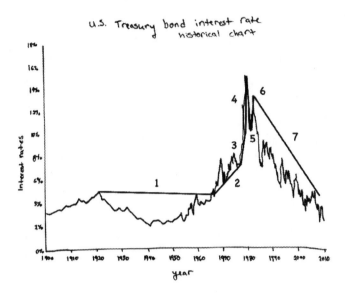

U.S. Treasury Bond Interest Rates

The hyperwave in interest rates occurred as a result of the United States defaulting on its debt, which happened on August 15, 1971, when President Richard Nixon closed the gold window.

Since 1971 there has been a parabolic increase to the M1 and M2 money supply. We believe this is the macroeconomic shift that provided the catalyst for the record number of hyperwaves that followed, and that is why it is considered the most important hyperwave that has ever occurred.

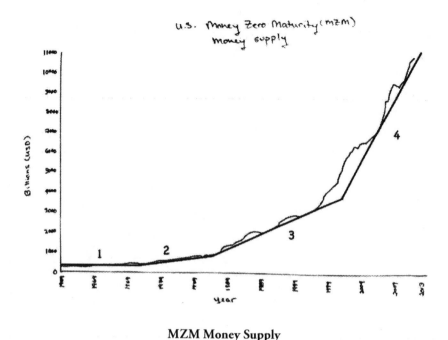

MZM Money Supply

When more money comes into the world, in a sound manner or not, it needs to be allocated into a limited supply of assets. When an exponential amount of capital is being added to a finite supply of assets, then it would follow that the assets proceed to grow in an exponential manner.

This never seems like a problem during the growth phase. Only in hindsight are we able to understand many of the consequences that are a by-product of unsustainable growth.

We propose this question: if money supply was flat or increasing in a linear fashion, then would hyperwaves be as prevalent as they currently are?

The rest of the world rebelled because the US dollar was the reserve currency, and if the US was inflating, then that means it is diminishing in value in regard to gold and other currencies; hence, the severe and immediate inflation of commodities.

It is important to note that period in time was very unusual, as is the current environment.

Remember that before a hyperwave begins to form, we know what it will look like before it completes. The irresponsible actions of the 1960s and 1970s catalyzed the hyperwaves that resulted over the following fifty to sixty years, and we are far from the terminal points.

The current macroeconomic environment is a result of monetary policies that are a half century old. Similar to phase 1 of a hyperwave, or a geyser, the longer that the pressure is allowed to build up, the more destructive the inevitable explosion will be.

Those charts are meant to help the reader visualize the underlying problem that has led to the tectonic shift that is occurring beneath our feet. They were chosen to illustrate the problem, but the fact that they are also hyperwaves is more than a coincidence.

If the economic shift (leaving the gold standard) results in a multitude of hyper-waves, then it is logical that the shift itself (money supply) also takes on the form of a hyperwave.

Hyperwaves are not sustainable regardless of if they occur in equities, commodities, interest rates, or monetary supply. While it may seem like there is no end in sight for the fiat money system that has plagued the world since 1971, we believe there will be an equal and opposite reaction. If that does happen, then the result will see the globe returning to a sound money system.

The large majority of economists do not believe that will ever happen, but we are entirely unconvinced. The average fiat currency has a life expectancy of twenty-seven years.

At the time of this writing, it has been forty-eight years since Nixon closed the gold window and essentially forced us into a world of fiat currency. We have outlasted the large majority of previous attempts and are close to doubling the average life span. Nevertheless, it remains an unsustainable structure and we are confident that history will eventually repeat itself.

PHASE 4

TYPES OF HYPERWAVES

CHAPTER 15

FUNKY HYPERWAVES

Approximately one-fifth of hyperwaves will morph into funky hyperwaves by finding support at phase 2 or phase 3 and then creating a new all-time high. The textbook example of this deformity is the Nasdaq 100 over the past three decades.

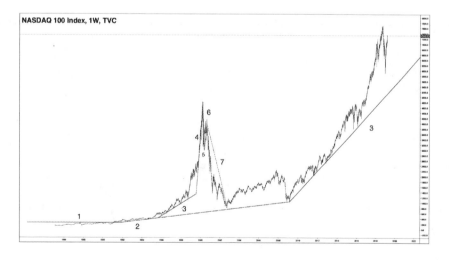

Nasdaq Funky Hyperwave

At the time, funky hyperwaves had not yet been discovered by Tyler. He was calling for a return to phase 1 and was forced to eat some crow after the market did not comply. The mortgage crisis of 2008 appeared to be the perfect catalyst to send the price down to his target. When that did not happen, he was left without an explanation.

Fortunately for him, the hyperwave pattern was not the only tool in his toolbelt. Instead of stubbornly staying on the sidelines while waiting for a return to phase 1, he whipped out his other most trustworthy apparatus, Consensio, and started to reenter long exposure shortly after the bottom was found.

Not until years later when he was studying the price of Bitcoin did he start to theorize about funky hyperwaves. Phase lines are extremely resilient in both bull and bear markets, but the creator of hyperwave theory had yet to consider the possibility of either phase 2 or phase 3 providing the strength that is needed to reverse a phase 7 before it reaches the second terminal point.

After realizing that this is possible, he began to find numerous other examples, the first of which is Dow Chemical from the 1930s. There were numerous hyperwaves in the early 1900s, and almost all returned to phase 1 during the Great Depression. However there was at least one company that temporarily avoided this fate.

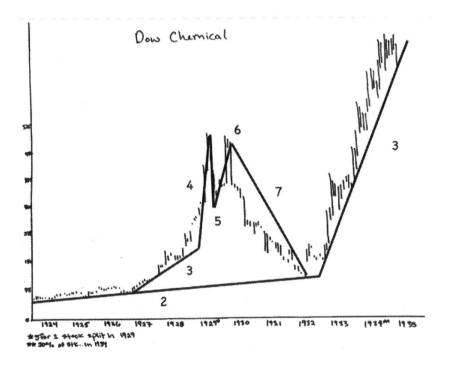

Dow Chemical

Dow Chemical took an alternative route after it found support at phase 2 and went on to create a new all-time high. It would be easy to view this as tremendously positive for the stock. We are not so convinced. Shirking the phase 7 target and creating a new all-time high appears to do nothing more than delaying the inevitable.

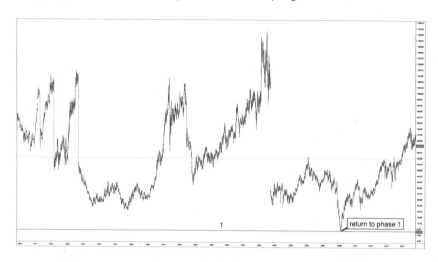

DowDupont, Formerly Known as Dow Chemical, Returns to Phase 1 in 2009

It took Dow Chemical eighty years, and a new name, before returning to phase 1. This is a great example of why funky hyperwaves may do little to alter the destination following the breakdown of phase 4.

It is important to note that this is not inflation-adjusted. Even though $6.00 is worth drastically less now than it was one hundred years ago, price still returned to the dollar amount that constituted the century-old phase 1.

The hyperwave is not complete until it reaches the terminal phase 1, regardless of whether or not it takes a funky route. After the hyperwave is complete, then the market is free to proceed in whichever direction it so pleases. It can continue falling, it can consolidate for a prolonged period, or it can find the support that is needed to spur on a new bull market. There will eventually be an exception to this pattern; however, it is important to keep in mind how long it can take to return to phase 1 before assuming that an exception has been found.

That is a very frightening implication when one considers the major indices that are currently in a hyperwave and where the respective phase 1's await.

Major Indices That Are Currently in a Hyperwave with Respective Phase 1's:

Index	Current Phase	Phase 1
S&P 500	3	$139
Nasdaq 100	3 (funky)	$241.50
Value Line Index	3	$311.32

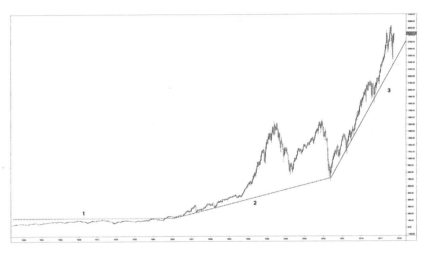

S&P 500 Hyperwave

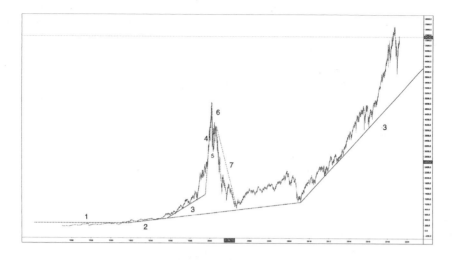

Nasdaq 100 Hyperwave

Value Line Index Hyperwave

It is hard to imagine the repercussions of these major indices returning to phase 1. Such low targets will always seem inconceivable while the market(s) remains in phase 3 or phase 4. If this seems impossible, then it is very important to start with an understanding that the markets have a strong tendency to make the unthinkable a reality.

It is also important to understand the fundamental factors that preceded these enormous moves. The major run-up in the US equity markets started to occur almost immediately after President Nixon closed the gold window. These events are so close in proximity that it is very hard to conclude that it is simply a coincidence.

The world was flooded with funny money shortly after the last link to sound money was removed. Keynesian economists[19] will laud this as the greatest economic accomplishment of the century, and their praises are all based on the unfounded assumption that more money supply equals more wealth.

We are not inclined to agree with this concept and instead have the perspective that more money supply equals more inflation. This only appears like a good thing while the music is still playing and asset prices are still appreciating.

The music that is playing is far less soothing to those that have studied history and know that every single fiat currency the world has ever known eventually collapsed to $0. Following World War I, the Treaty of Versailles required the Weimar Germany Republic to pay war reparations to the allied nations. Their response was to print currency that was not backed by anything in order to cover the tab. This caused hyperinflation, and when the country replaced the Papiermark with the Rentenmark[20], the exchange rate was one for 1 trillion.

There are numerous other modern examples, including but not limited to the Argentinian peso, the Zimbabwe dollar, the Peru sol, and the Chilean escudo. Unfortunately, this is not just a modern phenomenon. When France attempted to convert to "coin-backed" paper currency in the 1700s, the powers that be continued to increase the money supply until the paper franc lost 99 percent of its value in twelve years. The orchestrator of this

---

[19] Keynesian Economics is an economic theory developed by the British economist John Maynard Keynes during the 1930s that advocates for increased government expenditures and lower taxes to stimulate demand to prevent economic recessions.

[20] Recommended reading: "Die Reichbank 1876 bis 1945," in: *Fünfzig Jahre Deutsche Mark, Notenbank und Währung in Deutschland seit 1948*, Deutsche Bundesbank, ed. (München: Verlag C. H. Beck, 1998), pp. 29 – 89, esp. pp. 46 – 54; C. Bresciani-Turroni, *The Economics of Inflation, A Study of Currency Depreciation in Post-War Germany* (Northampton: John Dickens & Co., 1968 [1931]); also F.D. Graham, *Exchange, Prices, And Production in Hyper-Inflation: Germany, 1920 – 1923* (New York: Russell & Russell, 1967 [1930]).

shift to fiat currency, John Law, even went so far as to proclaim, "A banker deserved death if he made issues without having sufficient security to answer all demands.[21]"

For a short time, the paper currency issued by Law & Co floated at a significant premium to the government coinage. This is due to his promise to make all notes payable at sight and in the coin current at the time they were issued. While a thousand livres of silver might be worth its nominal value on the day it was issued, they were subject to constant debasement at the hands of the unscrupulous French government. Law promised to redeem his paper notes for the original value of the coinage.

Eventually John Law's bank became so profitable that it was deemed unsuited for the private sector and the royal establishment soon monopolized the industry. Law was either unwilling or unable to stop the regent from eventually fabricating these notes in order to add to his personal coffers. The blame for the fraudulent increase in money supply often falls upon John Law, but that may be unwarranted.

> As soon as the bank, from a private, became a public institution, the Regent caused a fabrication of notes to the amount of one thousand millions of livres. While the affairs of the bank were under his [John Law's] control the issues had never exceeded sixty million.[22]

Instead of placing the blame on John Law for the eventual currency collapse, it could be said that he was the only honest and responsible individual who has ever been in control of a nation's fiat money supply. Under his control, the amount of paper money never increased, and if the historical accounts are to be believed, he always maintained sufficient security to answer all demands. Shortly after the monarch took control, the entire system collapsed.

Even the Roman Empire was unable to avoid a complete currency collapse when it devalued the denarius from 100 percent pure silver down to 0.05 percent. During the heyday of Rome, it would have been nearly impossible for citizens to imagine that the

---

[21] MacKay C. (1841) *Extraordinary Popular Delusions and the Madness of Crowds.* United Kingdom: Pantianos Classics

[22] MEMOIRS OF EXTRAORDINARY POPULAR DELUSIONS. (n.d.). Retrieved from https://www.gutenberg.org/files/636/636-h/636-h.htm

entire empire could collapse. Only after the fact would this extremely unlikely possibility become inevitable.

It is worth noting that the 0.05 percent silver that backed the denarius during its nadir is 5 percent more backing than the world currencies currently have. After understanding the sobering reality of fiat currency, it becomes relatively easy to believe that the modern economy can suffer a similar fate.

The major indices broke through phase 1 shortly after the world transitioned to a fiat monetary system. History has proven that fiat money and hyperwaves are unsustainable. Both will hyperinflate before returning to whence they came. If the S&P 500, Dow Jones Industrial Average, and Value Line Index eventually return to phase 1, then prices will return to levels when the money supply was backed by gold. Therefore, returning to a sound monetary system could be what causes the major indices to deflate back to those levels.

Returning to a sound money standard could send the global economy into a tailspin before it eventually recovers and ripping off that Band-Aid could be exactly what causes the major indices to return to phase 1. That would undoubtedly be the biggest meltdown that the world has ever experienced, but we believe it would pave the way for a much brighter future provided that it results in the world returning to a sound money standard.

The world entered into the dark ages after the collapse of Rome's fiat currency. After recovering we eventually transitioned into a great period of renaissance, which didn't start to take place until the fourteenth century after Florence returned to the gold standard.

CHAPTER 16

FUNKY FRACTALS A.K.A. NESTED HYPERWAVES

Fractal: any of various extremely irregular curves or shapes for which any suitably chosen part is similar in shape to a given larger or smaller part when magnified or reduced to the same size.[23]

Hyperwave theory all but disregards similar shapes that occur on time frames that are less than weekly charts. Nevertheless, this pattern has been observed on time frames from the monthly down to the one-minute chart. When hyperwave fractals, or funky fractals, occur on lower time frames, there can be a lot of money to be made by applying the same rules.

First, it is important to understand that some rules and percentages are not nearly as reliable. For example, if a funky fractal breaks down the fourth phase, then it is not nearly as likely to return to phase 1.

Furthermore, we do not know the likelihood of phase 2 or phase 3 completing the pattern on lower time frames as we do with the weekly pattern. As long as one understands that shorter time frames are less reliable, then it is certainly okay to trade these fractals similarly.

---

[23] Fractal. (n.d.). Retrieved from https://www.merriam-webster.com/dictionary/fractal

Funky hyperwaves are not to be confused with funky fractals. The former takes place after a normal hyperwave breaks down phase 4 and then creates a new all-time high after finding support at phase 2 or phase 3. A funky fractal is a smaller version of a traditional hyperwave, whereby the seven phases occur on a timescale that is shorter than the weekly.

If the pattern occurs on the one-minute, one-day, or any other time frame in between, then it is a funky fractal. If the pattern occurs on the weekly and breaks down phase 4 then creates a new all-time high after finding support from phase 2, then it is a funky hyperwave.

Hyperwaves are very rare; funky hyperwaves will only develop in one out of five hyperwaves and funky fractals appear to be the scarcest of all. The Nasdaq 100 is a great example of a funky hyperwave, and the Turkish lira is a beautiful representation of a funky fractal.

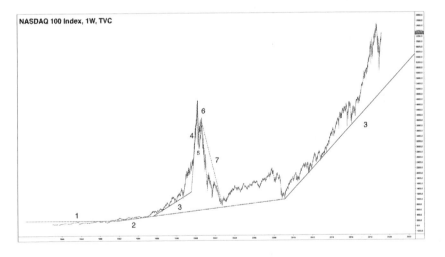

Nasdaq Funky Hyperwave

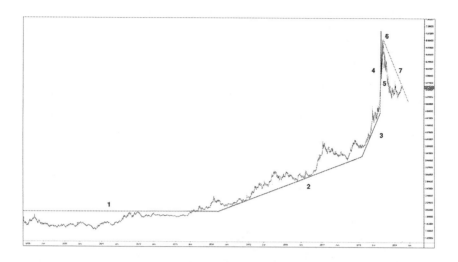

Turkish Lira Funky Fractal on the Daily Chart

The fourth to seventh phases are textbook. The close below phase 4 provided an ideal area to take profit, and the phase 6 bounce provided a perfect shorting opportunity; we will delve into shorting strategies later in this book. However, this is also an example of why it can be a mistake to be overly focused on the shorter time frames.

The daily funky fractal appears as though phase 3 has been violated; therefore, a return to phase 2 is to be expected. However, zooming out to the weekly chart paints a different picture. When using weekly candles, phase 3 is drawn differently, and that could turn out to be a crucial difference.

Turkish Lira Hyperwave Using Weekly Chart

The weekly chart appears as though phase 3 is just getting started. The daily chart makes it look like phase 7 has already broken down phase 3. In this case, we should disregard the daily and stick to the weekly chart. This does not mean that the weekly interpretation will necessarily be right. It does mean that the higher time frames always take precedence over the lower time frames.

We have recently seen funky fractals form in Bitcoin as well as Palladium.

Bitcoin

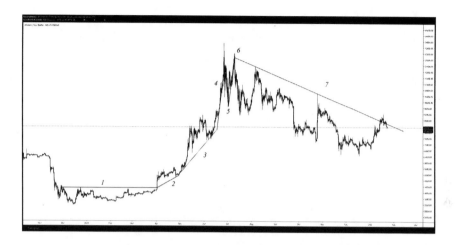

Bitcoin Funky Fractal

Palladium

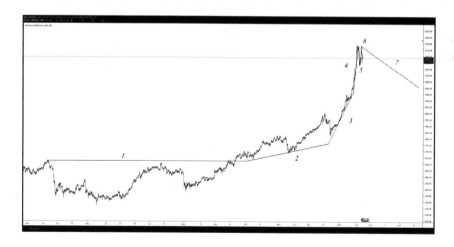

Palladium Funky Fractal

CHAPTER 17

REPEATING HYPERWAVES

Funky fractals also should not be confused with repeating hyperwaves. A repeating hyperwave occurs when the first one completes all seven phases, on the weekly chart, and then goes on to form a second hyperwave after returning to phase 1. This is also extremely rare but within the realm of possibilities. General Electric is the prime example of a repeating hyperwave. It formed the most perfected hyperwave that we have ever seen in the early 1900s.

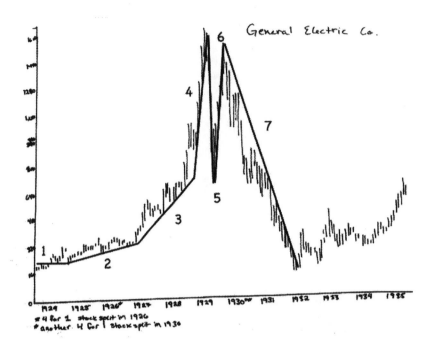

General Electric Company Perfected Hyperwave

Following the completion of the original hyperwave, it formed another phase 1 that took more than forty years to develop. Phase 2 started in the 1980s after price broke through the horizontal resistance at $1.50. Phases 3–7 followed relatively shortly thereafter.

General Electric Current Hyperwave

Back-to-back, or repeating hyperwaves are entirely distinct from funky hyperwaves and funky fractals because they follow the standard archetype and return to phase 1 before starting the second pattern. Funky hyperwaves do not return to phase 1. Instead, they find support at phase 2 or phase 3 before creating a new all-time high. Funky fractals follow the traditional pattern but do it on a smaller time frame than the weekly. This makes them tradeable as hyperwaves but less reliable. Repeating hyperwaves are two distinct iterations of the same pattern; therefore, both are expected to honor the traditional rules.

CHAPTER 18

COMPARING HYPERWAVES TO ELLIOTT WAVES

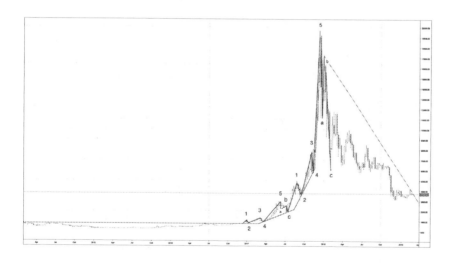

Hyperwave Phase Lines with Elliott Waves

Introduction to Elliott Wave Theory

Elliot waves were developed by E. N. Elliott and were later popularized by Robert Prechter and A. J. Frost in the book *Elliott Wave Principle: Key to Market Behavior*[24].

---

[24] Frost, A. and Prechter, R. (1977). *Elliott Wave Principle: Key to Market Behavior.*

The most elementary way to think of Elliott waves is through the basic 5 wave sequence, which is followed by the basic 3 wave correction.

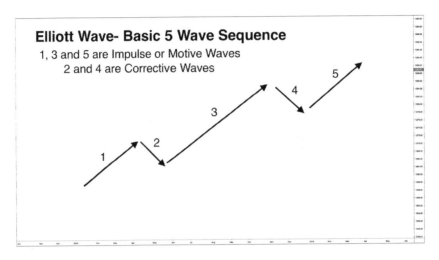

Elliott Wave: Basic 5 Wave Sequence

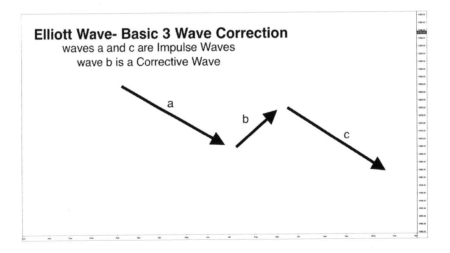

Elliott Wave: Basic 3 Wave Correction

Hyperwave theory should not be confused with the principles of Elliott waves. Without a nuanced understanding of hyperwaves, this could be very easy to do, especially if one was introduced to Elliott waves first.

Through making this distinction, we are in no way attempting to disparage or discount Elliott Wave principles. The authors of this book have great respect for the work that was done by E. N. Elliott, and the mastermind behind hyperwave theory, Tyler, has had the pleasure of comparing the two theories in depth with none other than Robert Prechter.

Both noticed a few small similarities before concluding that hyperwave is unique in its own right.

The Elliott impulse or motive waves (1, 3, and 5) appear similar to phase 2, 3, and 4 of a hyperwave. Furthermore, it may also be easy to confuse wave A with phase 5, wave B with phase 6, and wave C as phase 7.

There are many reasons why this is not true, and we will do our best to help readers understand the difference.

The first two major differences are related to the frequency at which they occur as well as the all-important first phase of a hyperwave.

According to Elliott Wave theory, every asset is always in an Elliott Wave, and that is true on every scale.

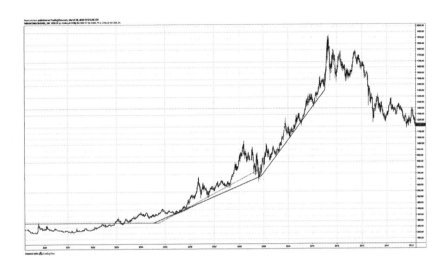

Elliott Wave Cycles and Fractals

The theory states that every time frame is in perpetual Elliott Wave fractals. If looking at the one-minute chart then observing the minute cycles, if zoomed out to the weekly, monthly, or yearly then viewing cycles and supercycles. All are expected to simultaneously form the same pattern on different time scales.

This is the first important difference between hyperwaves and Elliott Waves. Hyperwaves are extremely rare, and through history, less than 1 percent of assets have ever experienced a confirmed hyperwave. What is even rarer than hyperwaves are funky fractals, which are hyperwave patterns on shorter time frames than the weekly.

Once an asset enters a hyperwave, it is extremely rare for smaller time frames to form hyperwave fractals. This is in direct contrast to Elliott wave theory.

Another important distinction to make is that all hyperwaves are bubbles, and very few Elliott Waves are bubbles. Elliot Waves are expected to occur in all markets at all times, and bubbles are extremely rare by comparison.

Hyperwave is a specific subsection of bubbles. While bubbles are rare, hyperwaves are even more so. The frequency at which hyperwaves occur relative to Elliott waves is a very important distinction.

Phase 1

Perhaps the single most important practical difference between the two theories is phase 1. Hyperwave states that phase 1 is the most important phase of the pattern, whereas Elliott Waves do not have anything similar to a phase 1.

The reason phase 1 is so important is because it is building up the necessary pressure for the eruption that follows, and it provides the target which price is expected to return to before phase 7 is complete.

Angles of Phases

Another very important distinction to make is the angle of the phase lines. You will notice in the sequences above that waves 1, 3, and 5 are all occurring at a similar angle, and this is never true with hyperwaves.

Phase 2 always occurs at a thirty- to forty-five-degree angle.
Phase 3 always occurs at a forty-five- to sixty-degree angle.
Phase 4 always occurs at a sixty- to ninety-degree angle.

The difference in phase lines angles is a crucial element of identifying hyperwaves and the respective phases. Even if the structure of a chart looks similar to the archetype, it will not qualify if all the angles do not fit into those ranges.

Elliott wave theory does not account for varying angles.

Support and Resistance

Another key differentiator is the fact that phase lines are all crucial areas of support and resistance while Elliott Wave lines are not. Impulse waves do not indicate support, and corrective waves do not act as resistance.

In hyperwaves, phases 1, 5, and 7 are resistance, while phases 2, 3, 4, and 6 are supported. This is a crucial aspect of hyperwave theory because it is how one can identify entry and exit points as well as stop-losses. The best way to trade hyperwaves is to buy at or near the trend line that represents phase 3 and to sell as soon as a weekly candle closes below phase 3 or phase 4.

Remember that only 85 percent of phase 3's go on to complete the next four phases; therefore, a close below phase 3 indicates an area to execute a stop-loss. This is very different from how Elliott waves are identified and traded.

<u>Return to Phase 1</u>

Both theories also have different perspectives about the corrective phases. Hyperwave states that the price will return to phase 1 after entering phase 7, whereas Elliot Waves expect the ABC correction to find support above the first wave.

There are many differences, and phase 1 is perhaps the most important aspect. Returning to phase 1 after breaking down phase 4 is at the heart of hyperwave theory. This is what has allowed Tyler to not only sell the top of all the major asset bubbles over the past thirty years but also to prepare for what followed. Selling the top of a bubble is only the first step to retaining profits. The next step is knowing not to buy back in during phase 7, and the last step is understanding how the phase 7 will impact other markets.

Hyperwaves are like snowflakes. They all share very similar characteristics, but no two are identical. To understand what constitutes as a snowflake, it is important to clarify what is not a snowflake. Raindrops are not snowflakes and the differences are clear.

Elliott waves are like raindrops.

Once the rain turns into hail, it can be more difficult to differentiate the characteristics from a snowflake. In this situation, parabolic curves and hyperwave deformities, with too many or not enough phases, are similar to hail.

We will use a spectrum to help distinguish legitimate hyperwaves from imposters. On one end of the spectrum is the most perfected hyperwave that has ever existed. On the other end of the spectrum is the sloppiest pattern which barely meets all the requirements. Outside of the spectrum are the patterns that are very close to being included inside the sloppier end, but are left out due to failure to conform with the guidelines.

PHASE 5

HYPERWAVE SPECTRUM

CHAPTER 19

OUTSIDE THE SPECTRUM

Gold

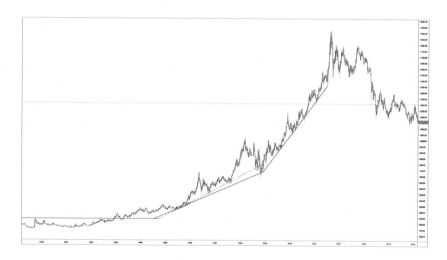

Gold Trend Lines

On the surface, gold looks like a hyperwave, but it is barely outside the spectrum of what qualifies. Phase 2 is a major problem. It would be very generous to disregard the top phase 2 line (dotted blue) that has six touch points in favor of the solid blue line that only has two touch points.

Phase 4 is also a problem. It is about the weakest phase 4 that you will ever see in relation to the prior three phases. The biggest problem is that a parabola is a much better fit. Hyperwaves are always linear patterns that are drawn with trend lines. However, that does not imply that all parabolic advances are hyperwaves.

When struggling to find the right phase lines, as we do here with the second and third, it can often be the case that a parabola is the best fit. When the pattern is more of a curve than angular, it suggests that the asset in question likely is not a hyperwave. A short fourth phase, in relation to the second and third, is another strong indication that a parabola is the best fit.

This is important, mostly because of the target that results from a breakdown. A violated parabola calls for an 85 percent retrace while hyperwave calls for a return to phase 1, which is usually more in the order of a 95 percent retracement.

All hyperwaves are bubbles; not all bubbles are hyperwaves.
All parabolas are bubbles; not all bubbles are parabolas.

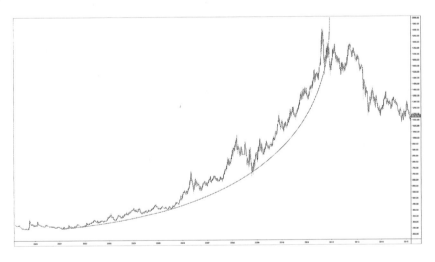

Gold Parabola

Litecoin

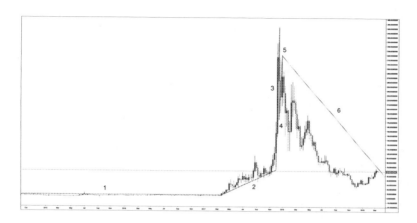

Litecoin: Not a Hyperwave

Litecoin is not a hyperwave, for one specific reason. There is no phase 3. All hyperwaves have seven phases. Similar to funky fractals, something like Litecoin could have been traded like a hyperwave, but that doesn't necessarily mean that it is one. The pieces are put together to create a very similar pattern, but it is missing a very important part, and that is the third phase. This is an unacceptable deformity.

Intuitive Surgical, Inc.

Intuitive Surgical, Inc. (NASDAQ: ISRG) Trend Lines

Is ISRG a hyperwave that is currently nearing the top of phase 6? We are getting closer, but this still looks a little too suspect to have confidence that it will conform to the rules of hyperwave, specifically those that follow a phase 4 breakdown.

Phase 1 looks good, and phase 2 did a perfect job of catching the 2009 meltdown by connecting the phase 1 breakout with the first major correction. So far so good. Phases 3 and 4 are where it gets weird.

Phase 3 is too generous. One would have had to draw it three different times from 2011 to 2014. That is not necessarily a problem if it had more touch points. Every other phase 3 trend line has at least three touch points, and every one was violated. The only way to keep this phase 3 valid is to adjust it down until there are only two touch points. In general, the phase line needs to have at least three touch points. This is not a necessity, but it is something to consider. When there are three possible trend lines, two with three touch points and one with two touch points, then it is overly ambitious to use the one with only two touches.

All closes need to be above phases 2, 3, 4, and 6. However, that doesn't mean we should make adjustments in hindsight to conform to the rules. Sometimes a valid phase 3 gets a weekly close below and then continues to rally.

When trading hyperwaves, it is simply not prudent to continually adjust phase lines each time the prior one gets violated. If this was the approach, then how would one know when the phaseline is violated versus when it is time to simply make another adjustment? The number of touch points is very important. It can be feasible to adjust the trend line down and wait on the sidelines to see how it develops. When the price never returns to test the new trend line, then that is a strong indication that it is not drawn accurately. If price did retest that area before establishing phase 4, then it would be a much different story.

It is within the rules to adjust a phase line after a weekly candle closes below that original line that was penciled in. However, it is very important to get confirmation by waiting for more touch points after it is drawn. If that doesn't happen, then one should proceed with caution and suspicion.

Furthermore phase 4 does not come together at an apex with the third. It is okay to use some wiggle room, but this is more than just a small deviation. The more you wiggle away from the archetype, the less likely it is to conform to the rules. This current rally could take out the highs of the apparent phase 4. If that were to happen, some may say that this is the first phase 6 to exceed the phase 4 all-time high. They would have a lot of good reasons to draw that conclusion, but we would disagree and again point to the parabola pattern. A curved line appears to be a much better fit, and this is another one that we would leave outside of the spectrum, but just barely.

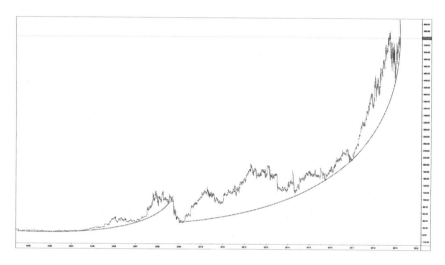

Intuitive Surgical, Inc. (NASDAQ: ISRG) Parabolas

Analog Devices, Inc.

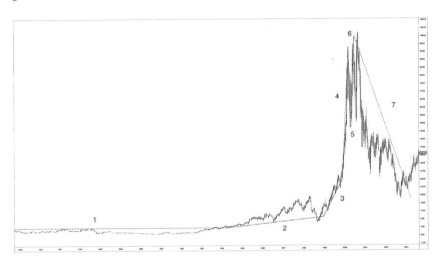

Analog Devices, Inc. (NASDAQ: ADI)

Is Analog Devices the first phase 6 that created a new all-time high above phase 4, not once but twice? This is about as close as they get, but there was one major reason to be suspicious of this in real time, and that is phase 2.

We have an established phase 2 with five touch points, and then it gets violated for seven straight weekly closes. It would simply be too generous to redraw it with two touch points, especially due to how close it came to returning to phase 1. That would be a very narrow angle, which is not necessarily a deal breaker if it had more touch points.

In many scenarios, it is possible to trade a deformity with the traditional rules of hyperwave, but that is not always the case. If you decided to short phase 6 as it was approaching the prior all-time highs, like one may be inclined to do with ISRG at the time of this writing, then you would have gotten brutally stopped out right before the major sell-off.

When there are so many active hyperwaves, one should focus on finding patterns that are as close to the archetype as possible because those are the ones most likely to respect the rules.

2013–2015 Bitcoin

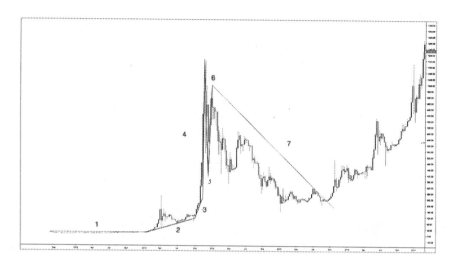

Bitcoin 2013–2015

On the surface, it looks like a hyperwave, and if that is the case, then it is the first ever hyperwave to break down phase 2 without returning to phase 1.

This is very close, but it is still outside the realm of what can be labeled a hyperwave. Phase 3 is so small that it is nonexistent for all intents and purposes. It does come together at a rather nice apex, and it does create a nice angle with the second phase. Nevertheless, price does not exceed the high of phase 2. An apparent phase 3 that fails to create a new all-time high is no phase 3 at all and would be considered an extension of phase 2.

Therefore, it only has six total phases, similar to Litecoin, and that is enough to put it outside of the spectrum. Breaking down phase 2 and failing to return to phase 1 is not a problem because it is not a hyperwave.

Cisco Systems, Inc.

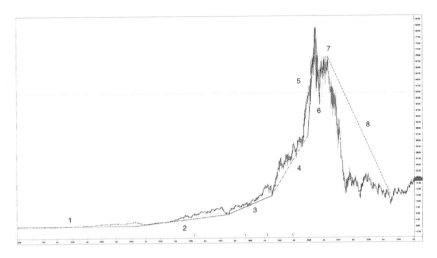

Cisco Systems, Inc. (NASDAQ: CSCO) Has an Extra Phase

Cisco is not a hyperwave because it has an extra phase. Litecoin and 2013–2015 Bitcoin failed to qualify because they lacked a valid phase 3. Cisco has the opposite problem of having one too many bull phases.

It would be possible to fudge the second and third phases to fit the guidelines, but that is more liberty than we wish to take. The five phases to the upside fit too perfectly to disregard. The apexes are beautiful, each has a good number of touch points, and the angles all progress in such a manner that each phase deserves to be distinguished from the prior.

All hyperwaves have seven phases. Ones that have six or eight can be traded with similar rules, but they are not hyperwaves.

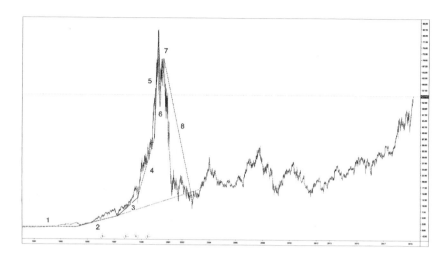

Cisco Systems, Inc. Phase 2 Breakdown

When zooming out, we will notice the importance of making this distinction. Notice that the price broke down the phase 2 trend line for months but failed to return to phase 1. Price hasn't yet created a new all-time high, but that is what appears most likely moving forward.

When there are this many active hyperwaves, it is prudent to be as picky as possible. Many candidates will be borderline, and mislabeling something as a hyperwave is much riskier than making the opposite mischaracterization.

If one does not label a borderline pattern as a hyperwave and is incorrect in the assessment, then that person only costs himself or herself opportunity. On the other hand, if one considers a borderline pattern as a valid hyperwave, then it could cost that person actual money if he or she is incorrect.

There are so many hyperwaves that it would be impossible to trade or invest in them all. Therefore, one would be wise to be as picky as possible when analyzing potential candidates. Look for the best opportunities possible, and do not waste too much time with examples that do not closely adhere to the archetype and limitations.

Ethereum ETHUSD

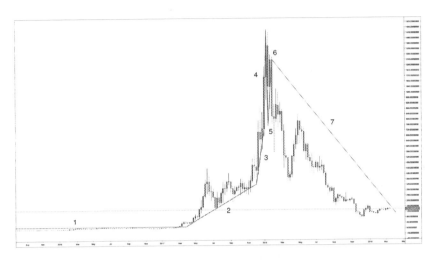

Ethereum (ETH)

Ethereum is standing on a razor's edge. It is very hard to put this outside the spectrum because it fits the archetype so nicely. Phase 1 is beautiful. The second, third, and fourth phases all have picture-perfect apexes. The angles are also on the mark. Phase 5 is short, as is phase 6, but that is okay.

Phase 7 has nearly returned to phase 1, and that would complete the pattern. The problem with this one is the amplitude and the duration. The previous largest hyperwave took place in the Japanese stock market during the 1980s, and it returned 4,000 percent from peak to valley.

Most hyperwaves return 800–2,000 percent, and that makes the Japanese equity hyperwave an anomaly. Bitcoin is the fastest-growing asset in the history of modern economics, and it couldn't even rival the ROI of the manipulated Japanese equity hyperwave, returning slightly under 2,000 percent during the 2017 hyperwave. On the other hand, Ethereum more than doubled the biggest hyperwave our seismograph has ever recorded, coming in at 8,896 percent while doing so in only forty-four weeks.

To call this a hyperwave would imply that it is the shortest in duration while also being the largest in amplitude by more than 2X. This would make it such an outlier that it would be way off on the edge of a heat map.

On the surface, it appears to adhere very closely to the archetype. However, it is very hard to consider this a hyperwave since it is so different from the rest of the snowflakes. All hyperwaves share very similar characteristics in regard to the formation, duration, and amplitude. Ethereum formed like a hyperwave, but the duration and amplitude are so different from the others that we chose to leave it slightly outside the spectrum.

This is as close as it gets to being a hyperwave. It is following the rules, but the duration and amplitude are very important factors for individual phases as well as for the pattern as a whole. If this was longer in duration or smaller in amplitude, then it would most likely qualify, but as it stands, we prefer to leave it oscillating towards the wrong side of the razor's edge.

CHAPTER 20

INSIDE THE SPECTRUM

Nasdaq

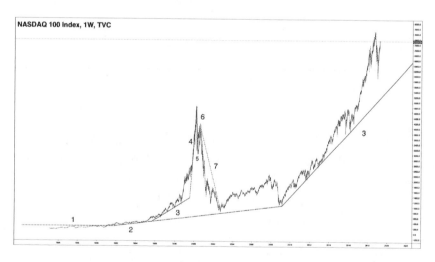

Nasdaq Funky Hyperwave

The Nasdaq experienced a very iffy hyperwave during the dot-com bubble. It was the first funky hyperwave that jived Tyler out of the return to phase 1 that he had been publicly calling for. It wiggles quite far away from the archetype, and that could be a reason why it decided not to respect the traditional rules.

Phase 1 and phase 2 are beautiful, but it gets suspect around phases 3 and 4. The apex between the two is so far off that it almost leaves room for an extra phase to the upside. Drawing an extra trend line gives us much nicer apexes, but it also gives us one too many phases.

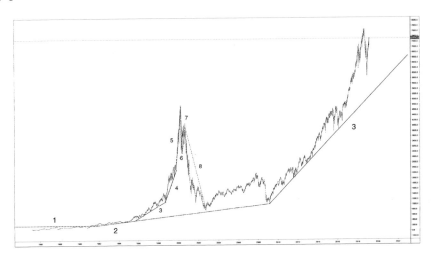

Nasdaq 8 Trend Lines

This is almost enough to leave it outside of the spectrum. It is borderline at best, and this would be a good example of when to proceed with caution. Adding the extra phase does improve the apexes, and there are enough touch points on the extra phase to consider it valid. However, just because the extra phase has enough touch points to make it valid does not mean that it would be necessary.

Drawing the Nasdaq with only seven phases does require a significant amount of wiggle room. It requires extending the phase 3 past the apex, and that creates a sloppy vertex with the following phase. Some may be okay with this; others might not. It all depends on how picky the individual prefers to be with his or her analysis.

It is perfectly okay for a borderline pattern to be labeled as a hyperwave by one person and not by another. In this situation, they could both be right. We strive to make the rules and guidelines as clear-cut as possible, but that is not always the case when analyzing charts in real time. This leaves a gray area that can be subjective.

In these scenarios, it is important to remain open-minded. The reader may decide that the Nasdaq should be outside the spectrum and that Ethereum deserves to take its place. That is perfectly reasonable and even encouraged. On this end of the spectrum, we are splitting hairs in order to delve into the intricacies so that the reader can judge borderline patterns for himself or herself.

All in all, this seems like a good place to start including borderline prospects into the spectrum. It is far from ideal, but there isn't quite enough for us to place it on the outside or even on the edge. On this end of the spectrum is the sloppiest pattern that we can still consider a hyperwave; on the opposite end is the pattern which most closely fits the archetype. The Nasdaq is quite possibly the sloppiest pattern that can be quantified as a hyperwave. Nevertheless, it leaves much to be desired and therefore would be an ideal candidate to disrespect the rules at some point down the road.

While this one did deny Tyler out of the return to phase 1, it did not keep him from exiting growth stocks at the top. At the time, he was the chief investment officer at Amnivest Capital Management and was fiduciary for more than a billion dollars of institutional money. This position came with many benefits but also many restrictions.

The maximum cash allocation that was contractually allowed was 5 percent, which meant that his hands were tied when the Nasdaq broke down phase 4. The most he could sell was 5 percent of the portfolio, and this meant he had to focus on sector rotation. Growth stocks drove the price action during the bull market, and Tyler correctly concluded they would give up the most during the bear market. Therefore, he moved out of growth, into value, and he did it at just the right time.

Very few professional money managers were able to capitalize on the best five years that the US stock markets have ever experienced. Some stayed away entirely and only missed out on opportunity cost. Most became overexposed and lost their shirts when the market reversed. Tyler capitalized on the upside and protected himself and his clients from the downside despite the oppressive guidelines that he was forced to follow. Shortly thereafter, the PS Ephron Database listed him in the top 99th percentile of money managers.

We are not naive enough to think that the ironclad rules of hyperwave will never be violated, and we fully understand that it is only a matter of time. Revealing the rules that Tyler spent a lifetime developing may or may not be what causes future deformities. Either way, there will be a hyperwave that fits inside the spectrum that fails to abide by the rules. There will be a phase 6 that creates a new all-time high above the fourth, or a phase 7 that fails to return to phase 1 after breaking down the second. This is inevitable, and it is most likely to occur with one that is on the messier end of the spectrum. The further one wiggles away from the archetype, the more likely it is to disrespect the rules. That is why we think it is so important to stick to the patterns that are closer to the more perfected end of the spectrum, especially when there are this many to choose from.

Tyler was miffed when the Nasdaq failed to return to Phase 1 after entering Phase 7. Only in hindsight did he realize that price found support at Phase 2 and as a result created a massive funky hyperwave.

Bethlehem Steel

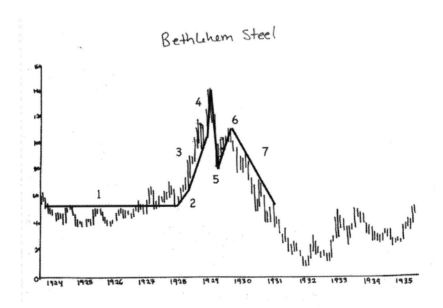

Bethlehem Steel Corp. Stocks (NYSE: BS)

Bethlehem Steel formed a very borderline hyperwave from 1924 - 1931. This one could just as easily be left outside the spectrum but we chose to include it primarily because we only have a monthly chart and believe it would be a better fit if it was a weekly chart.

Phase 1 is the primary cause for concern. Instead of price consolidating in a tight range over a long period of time we see consolidation happening it a wide range over a short period of time. As mentioned previously this isn't necessarily enough to disqualify it but it is a good reason to be concerned about the amplitude and duration of the following phases.

As it turns out any concerns would have been well founded. Phase 2 is so small that it is almost non-existent on the monthly scale. Phase 3 is solid and is followed by a weak Phase 4. The amplitude from the phase 1 breakout to the phase 4 peak is less than 150 percent which would make it the smallest hyperwave that we have ever seen in terms of amplitude.

Perhaps this one should be left outside the spectrum due to the sloppy Phase 1 and the relatively small move that followed, however phases five through seven are all strong reasons to keep it on the inside. The phase 6 bounce that followed phase 5 was textbook as was the return to phase 1.

As a result we have included this pattern in the sloppier end of the spectrum but our feelings wouldn't be hurt if others preferred to leave it out.

3M Co.

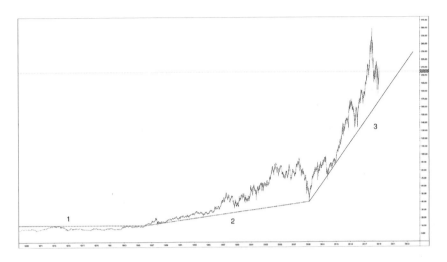

3M Co. (NYSE: MMM) Phase 3

3M is currently experiencing a hyperwave; that much is unquestionable. The apexes and angles are ideal. The reason why it is on the sloppier end of the spectrum is due to the price spending the majority of its time extended from the phase lines.

The most perfected hyperwave will see price sticking close to each phase, and that is not the case with 3M. Phase 2 spends the majority of its time well above the trend line. However, it returns to test the boundary before taking off into phase 3.

Since establishing the third phase, price has again shown its propensity to diverge from the trend line. It has not returned to retest phase 3 since 2012. It would be reasonable to draw in phase 4 after the pullback in 2015 failed to return to phase 3 and then proceeded to rally at a sharper angle than before.

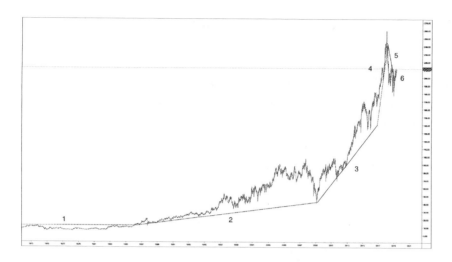

3M Could Be in Phase 6

This is a good illustration of how tricky it can be to label phases in real time, especially when price does not stick close to the phase lines. This is one that we would expect to follow the rules of hyperwave moving forward; however, it will be very difficult to trade due to the phases being somewhat ambiguous.

If phase 4 started in 2015, then this last pullback was phase 5 and the following bounce will qualify as phase 6. However, it is also entirely within reason to conclude that the 2015 run-up was simply an extension of phase 3, similar to what we saw with phase 2 from 2003 to 2007.

This is a good example of when to proceed with caution even though the asset is clearly in a hyperwave. When the phases are difficult to decipher, then it is important not to be overly confident in one's estimation.

The picture will become much clearer down the road; therefore, it would be best to wait for further confirmation. If it creates a new all-time high, then we can be confident 2015 was not phase 4 because phases 5 and 6 occur below the all-time high.

If this bounce creates a lower high and then goes on to close below phase 3, then we can be confident that 3M has entered phase 7 and a return to phase 2 would be highly likely. That would require a huge move, which would leave a large piece of the pie to capitalize on.

When there is room for a big move one way or the other, then it is a great time to wait patiently from the sidelines for further confirmation, and this is a prime example of such a situation.

Amazon.com, Inc.

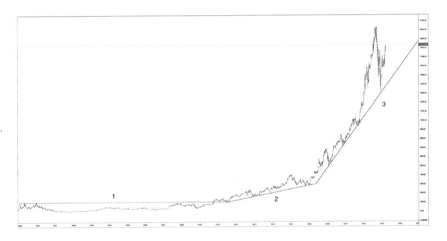

Amazon.com, Inc. (NASDAQ: AMZN) Hyperwave Phase 3

Amazon is in a hyperwave, but it finds itself in a similar situation as 3M. It is experiencing a hyperwave, but the current phase is ambiguous. Price sticks much closer to the trend lines, and that could help us to decide, but it still appears too early to be confident.

It is very difficult to decipher if phase 4 has already occurred. Price started taking off at a much steeper angle during the tail end of 2017 and a fourth phase could be drawn in. The angle and duration fit nicely, and this provides further confirmation that it was a real phase 4.

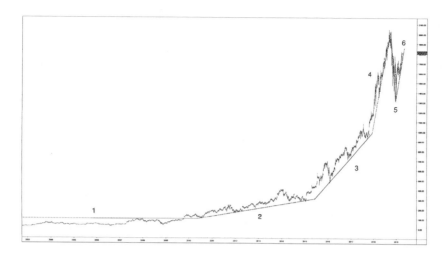

Amazon.com, Inc. (NASDAQ: AMZN) Hyperwave Phase 6

However, we have noticed that this is fairly common. The price will often become overextended from the phase line before establishing the next phase. Similar to what we saw with 3M at the latter part of phase 2. Price got significantly overextended before pulling back to retest phase 2, which provided so much support that the asset immediately entered phase 3.

Here we notice a big bounce from the phase 3 trend line. If this rally continues, then it could be the very beginning stages of phase 4. These situations can be very difficult to analyze in real time. However, sometimes it will represent a win/win scenario, and that was the case with Amazon.

Retesting phase 3 during the last couple weeks of 2018 provided a great buying opportunity regardless of how the phases were identified. If phase 4 already occurred, then the sell-off represented phase 5 and a phase 6 bounce is to be expected.

When an apparent phase 5 returns to phase 3, then it can represent a sort of win/win scenario. If it is phase 5, then this is an ideal area to get a phase 6 bounce. On the other hand, it is possible that the fourth phase was labeled incorrectly, which implies that the asset remains in phase 3. If that is the case, then it represents a great opportunity to buy at/near phase 3 with the plan to hold through phase 4.

In either situation, the price is expected to rally as opposed to continuing the sell-off. If it is still in phase 3, then that would be ideal, but if it is only a phase 6 bounce, then that should still be plenty profitable. Keep in mind there is always a very real chance that it breaks down phase 3 without bouncing. This can be viewed as a bit of a win/win situation; however, there is still a significant amount of risk associated with the entry.

This is a great illustration of how important it is for the price to stay relatively close to phase lines. When it diverges significantly, then it can be very difficult to identify the phases that follow.

Becton, Dickinson and Company

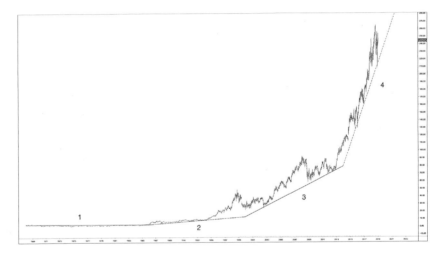

Becton, Dickinson and Company (NYSE: BDX) Phase 4

Becton, Dickinson and Company has established a beautiful phase 4, and it is much closer to the archetype than 3M or Amazon. Price does get overextended from the phase lines, specifically at the end of phase 2; however, that is the exception opposed to the rule.

The apexes leave a little bit to be desired, specifically between the second and third phases. However, it is still preferable to the previous charts because the current phase is indisputable.

It is currently in phase 4; there are no ifs, ands, or buts about it. Having a high level of confidence in regard to how the phases are labeled is crucial when trading or investing in real time. When a weekly candle closes below the phase 4 trend line, then one can be highly confident that the pattern will continue into the fifth, sixth, and seventh phases while understanding that there is a 20 percent chance that it turns into a funky hyperwave.

Being confident in how the price will proceed is a key to successfully beating the markets. Hyperwave projects how the price will proceed, but it will not always be possible to recognize in real time. When the current phase is dubious, like we see with Amazon and 3M, then it is impossible to be confident in how the price will progress.

On the other hand, when the current phase is as clear as day, then it is possible to plan accordingly. Finding patterns and phases that are indisputable should be the goal when analyzing hyperwaves. This will undoubtedly lead to a higher success rate than settling for more suspect patterns.

Abbott Laboratories

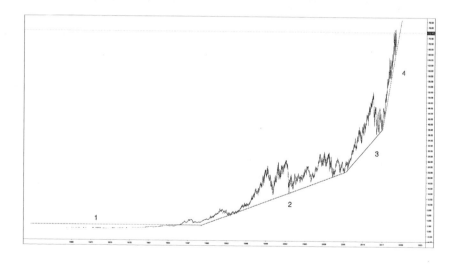

Abbott Laboratories (NYSE: ABT) Phase 4

Abbott Laboratories is another asset which has a well-established phase 4. The angles and apexes of each phase are wonderful. Price sticks relatively close to each trend line and leaves very little room for ambiguity.

However, this one leaves a little bit to be desired due to the proportions. The archetype calls for the following relationship: phase 1 is longer than phase 2, which is longer than phase 3, which is longer than phase 4.

Abbott Laboratories has a very short phase 3 followed by a massive phase 4. These proportions are not ideal, but that is not nearly enough to disqualify it. If phase 3 was longer, then this would be closer to the perfected end of the spectrum. Each snowflake will have characteristics that make it unique. Disproportionate third and fourth phases are primarily what make Abbott Laboratories special.

When questioning if a phase is long enough to be valid, it is important to consider the amplitude. If the all-time high of the new phase is approximately 50 percent, or more, greater than the prior phases all-time high, then that is enough. When it barely exceeds or doesn't at all, like with 2013–2015 Bitcoin, then it is likely too short.

We want to be wary of patterns that do not closely adhere to the archetype, and that is not necessary here. A slightly disproportionate phase 3 is not enough to question the integrity of this pattern moving forward.

Boeing Co.

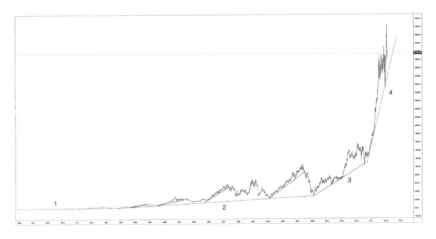

Boeing (NYSE:BA) Hyperwave

Boeing is experiencing an enormous hyperwave. The phases are clear-cut, but similar to Abbott Laboratories this one is lacking the ideal proportions. Phase 4 is as large as we have ever witnessed, as is the second. What is unique about this one is how many times phase 3 tried to establish itself before delivering the fourth phase.

There could be as many as five phase 3's drawn, and each time they broke down the price eventually found support at the original phase 2. This phase 3 is quite short, especially in relation to the others, but it does establish new all-time highs and creates beautiful apexes.

The fact that we can identify the current phase is very important. If this one adheres to the rules moving forward, and we have no reason to believe it won't, then it will have an unbelievably long way to fall just to return to phase 3, let alone phase 1.

S&P 500 SPX

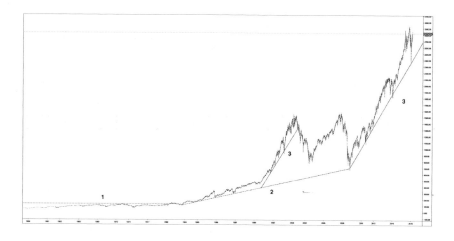

S&P 500 Hyperwave SPX

The S&P 500 is potentially developing the largest hyperwave the world has ever seen. Phase 1 is a century long and was violated shortly after President Nixon closed the gold window. Phase 2 is enormous and shows similarities to Boeing in the sense that establishing phase 3 took multiple attempts.

The price recently bounced strongly from phase 3, which started in 2009, and if it proceeds to establish a new all-time high in 2019, then it very well could enter the fourth phase. A conservative target would be $5,600 by 2023. A more aggressive target would be $7,500–$10,000 by 2025. Almost all phase 4's return 100 percent from phase 3's all-time high, and some return much more than that.

On the other hand, if it breaks down the phase 3 trend line, then the target would be a return to phase 2, which would likely be waiting in the $1,000 area. The common moral of this story is that hyperwaves and bubbles are not sustainable. The further they go up, the further they are expected to come down.

If the major US indices do enter a fourth phase—S&P 500, Dow Jones Industrial Average, Value line Index, and Nasdaq 100—then it is likely only going to have similar effects as a drug. A short-term high that is not worth the long-term effects.

If looking more than ten years down the road, then one should not be hoping that the major US indices enter the fourth phase. Unfortunately, the markets are highly influenced by politicians who operate with a one- to four-year time horizon, and the best thing that could happen in that amount of time is being able to take credit for the stock market doubling.

McDonald's

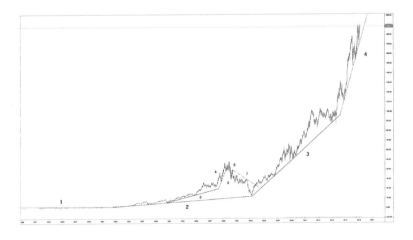

McDonald's Hyperwave (NYSE: MCD)

McDonald's is in the middle of a beautiful funky hyperwave. The original hyperwave occurred in the late 1990s during the dot-com bubble. The sell-off that followed found support at phase 2 and immediately went on to form a picture-perfect phase 3. Phase 4 started to establish itself during the spring of 2016, and it has been developing quite nicely ever since. The phases come together at perfect apexes. The duration, amplitude, and angles are also textbook.

Something interesting to note about the McDonald's funky hyperwave is the price action during the 2008 mortgage crisis. Price was close to the phase 3 trend line from 2006 to 2008, and that area of support held strong. As a result, there was not much room for a correction. When the rest of the markets were panic selling, McDonald's was stable. Instead of crashing, it simply formed a range that pushed the price toward the phase 3 trend line. After retesting that area for support, the bull run continued.

With hyperwaves that are this long in duration, it can be acceptable to use monthly candles instead of weekly.

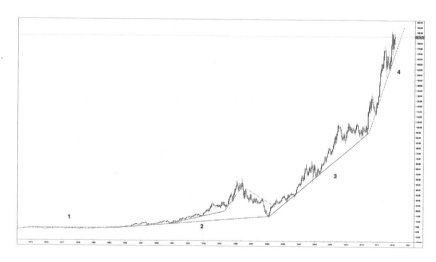

McDonald's Funky Hyperwave Monthly Chart (NYSE: MCD)

Using the monthly candles can be helpful when drawing the phase lines. It does not necessarily imply that one needs to wait until the end of the month to exit a position. If the pattern looks cleaner on a monthly chart, then it is more than okay to use the higher time frame to draw the phase lines. After that, one can zoom in to the weekly to time entries and exits. It is also possible to take signals from the monthly chart and disregard the weekly. It all comes down to preference. Technical analysis is an art; it is not a science.

2015 - 2020 Bitcoin

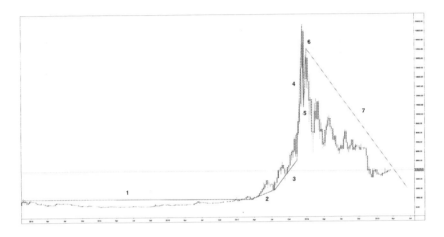

The Bitcoin Hyperwave

Bitcoin might deserve a higher place on the list since it is the reason why hyperwave was revealed to the public. Tyler was retired and had no interest in changing that anytime soon. He had moved onto a new occupation which he much preferred: head babysitter for his newly arrived grandson.

Then he received a call from yours truly (hey all, Leah here), who told him that Bitcoiners needed his help! The crypto sphere was in a catatonic state following the onset of phase 7, and nobody seemed to be taking profit.

In November 2017, everyone was ecstatic about Bitcoin crossing the five-figure threshold. Less than two months later, nobody could believe the price had fallen that low. I volunteered to quit my job, and Tyler agreed to come out of retirement. We have been public with our guidance with the hopes of guiding our audience and clients through the minefield that is phase 7 ever since.

Before partnering together to revamp Lucid Investment Strategies with a specialization in Bitcoin investments, Tyler had just finished closing the best trade of his illustrious career. He entered his full retirement account at $3,200 in August 2017 and sold at $12,500 in December 2017 for a return of nearly 400 percent in less than half a year. We started a YouTube channel, which we aptly named Hyperwave, where Tyler would talk through the Bitcoin hyperwave by providing real time analysis and predictions. That is when the other co-author came into the picture.

> Hello everyone, this is Tyler Coates a.k.a. Sawcruhteez. I joined Tyler Jenks and Leah at Lucid Investment Strategies as the lead financial analyst in early 2019. Hyperwave was gaining traction, and I began working directly with Tyler to trade and invest in assets that are in active hyperwaves for our clients. I also helped to develop training materials used for our workshops and webinars that have also served to write this book you're reading right now. Okay, let's get back to it.

Tyler's success trading Bitcoin went a long way to prove the effectiveness of hyperwave across different asset classes and different time periods. It worked in silver and sugar during the 1970s. It worked with interest rates and Japanese equities during the 80s. It worked with US stocks during the 2000s, and it worked with Bitcoin in 2017.

The reason that Bitcoin isn't higher on the spectrum is due to the duration as well as the apexes between the second, third, and fourth phases, all leaving a little bit to be desired. Nevertheless it has done more than enough to earn it's place on the totem pole.

At the time of this writing there are no known examples of a phase 7 that has failed to return to phase 1, after breaking down phase 2. It is important to note that Bitcoin cannot create a funky hyperwave at this juncture. Funky hyperwaves need to establish a new all-time high after finding support above phase 2 or phase 3. Bitcoin broke down phase 2 on November 12, 2018 when a weekly candle closed below.

It is entirely possible that Bitcoin will be the first asset that we know of to create a new all-time high without returning to phase 1 [despite having broken down phase 2]. If that happens it would do little to change the effectiveness of hyperwave theory.

In that scenario the strike rate of phase 7's that return to phase 1, after breaking down phase 2, would still be more than 99%. Furthermore the objective of hyperwave is to capitalize on the long side.

It is important to distinguish between making a call and taking a position. Tyler was very public about his call for Bitcoin to return to Phase 1 but he never took a short position. He did however use hyperwave theory to buy near the beginning of the 2017 parabolic move and sell near the top. If Bitcoin fails to return to phase 1 then it would do nothing to detract from the bottom line of the best trade Tyler ever made.

The world has Bitcoin to thank for hyperwave theory. If it were not for the former, then Tyler likely never would have revealed the latter.

Church and Dwight Co., Inc.

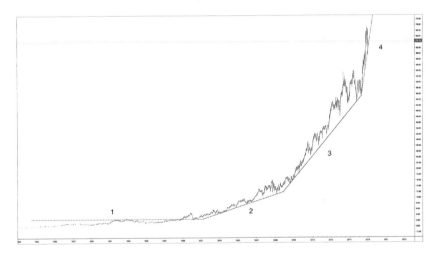

Church and Dwight Co., Inc. (NYSE: CHD) Phase 4

Church and Dwight is getting very close to the archetype. Phase 1 is long and has multiple touch points before breaking through. One small variation is that phase 2 did not create a perfect apex, and that is because the breakthrough from phase 1 threw back to retest prior resistance for support instead of creating a higher low. Not ideal but very acceptable.

Phase 2 more than makes up for it. The reason that it is ideal to have a perfect apex is that that means the phase line was drawn correctly the first time. In this situation, we would have only needed to draw it twice, and the second time was very reliable. Each time the trend line was tested, it provided an ideal entry. It is not considered a hyperwave until establishing phase 3; however, that doesn't mean one needs to pass on buying phase 2 when there is a very strong phase line intact.

Phase 3 is very similar. A strong trend line that is established early and price sticks very close to it throughout. Phase 4 is a perfect apex, and it is just starting as of April 2019. The only reason that this isn't higher on the list is that it isn't complete.

We would be very confident in this one abiding by the rules down the road; however, that has yet to happen. We wanted to include a few active hyperwaves in the spectrum but felt that the best examples should be reserved for those that have completed every phase.

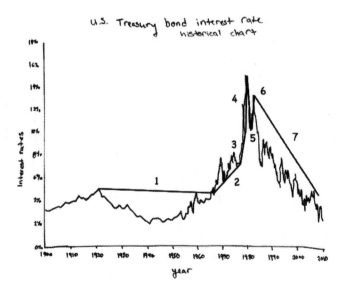

US Treasury Bond Interest Rate Hyperwave

While this may not be the single most perfected hyperwave that we have seen, it very well could be considered the single most important. That is because it directly catalyzed the large majority of hyperwaves that followed.

On 15 August 1971, the United States unilaterally terminated convertibility of the US dollar to gold, effectively bringing the Bretton Woods system to an end and rendering the dollar a fiat currency.[25]

Prior to the 1970s, the United States had never seen interest rates above 8 percent[26]. Interest rates skyrocketed in the 1970s and early 1980s, following the decision to remove the security backing the US dollar, and took on the form of a hyperwave. In 1980 it entered phase 3, and rates shot through 8 percent. By 1982 rates exceeded 15 percent after accelerating into phase 4.

High-interest rates are generally viewed as bearish for equities while being bullish for commodities. The stock market moved sideways during the 1970s. When the hyperwave in interest rates was reaching its peak, the S&P 500 was breaking out of a very long phase 1. This was not a coincidence at all.

Right as the hyperwave in interest rates entered phase 5, the US stock market was entering phase 2. When the interest rates entered the phase 6 bounce during the fall of 1987, the US stock market went the other direction. On October 19, 1987, the S&P 500 lost more than 20 percent in a single day, and that has been etched into history as Black Monday.

The sudden and sharp reversal of interest rates played a large part in the temporary turmoil, but phase 6 doesn't last long and phase 7 followed closely behind. As interest rates started to fall again, the stock market resumed its bull market. The hyperwave in interest rates that occurred in the 1970s and 1980s is the primary impetus for the hyperwaves that followed in both equities and commodities.

The interest rate hyperwave entered phase 7 in the late 1980s, and it promised to be a very long phase 7 indeed. The duration of phase 7 was a direct result of the length of the prior phases. Around this time, Tyler published a twenty-five-page article entitled "The Case for Bonds," and he called for rates to return to 6 percent when they were still above 12 percent.

---

[25] Annie Lowrey (9 February 2011) *End the Fed? Actually, Maybe Not.*, Retreived from https://slate.com/business/2011/02/ron-paul-vs-the-federal-reserve-does-he-really-want-to-end-the-fed.html
[26] Ritholtz, B (27 August, 2010) *History of US Interest Rates: 1790 - Present,* retrieved from https://ritholtz.com/2010/08/history-of-us-interest-rates-1790-present/

That call was entirely due to hyperwave theory, and it allowed him to predict what few others could believe at that time. It also allowed him to make a very valuable induction: a long phase 7 in interest rates should result in a long bull market in equities.

History provided strong validation for Tyler's expectations.

Stocks were flat from 1908 to 1920, due to spiking interest rates, and the Roaring Twenties began just as interest rates started to fall. Similarly, stocks were flat from 1970 to 1982 due to interest rates spiking. After interest rates fell we entered into an economy that is driven by bubbles: Black Monday, dot-com, sub-prime mortgages, and what is currently being deemed the *everything bubble*[27].

Returning to a sound monetary standard could be one outcome that drives the US indices back down to phase 1. Another possibility would be increasing interest rates that skyrocket back to double digits.

Nikkei 225

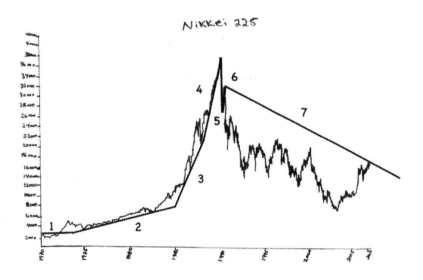

Nikkei 225 Hyperwave *

[27] Summers, G. (2017) The Everything Bubble. Scotts Valley, California: CreateSpace Independent Publishing Platform

Tyler developed hyperwave theory during the run-up in commodities that occurred in the 1970s. He implemented this newfound approach to predict the fall in interest rates that occurred in the 1980s. He also used it to sell the S&P 500 and Dow Jones Industrial Average in October 1987, one week before Black Monday. Shortly thereafter, he found himself amid the largest hyperwave that has ever occurred.

The Japanese equity bubble of the late 1980s returned 4,000 percent in sixteen years, which is more than twice as much as the previous largest hyperwaves. The manipulation that occurred during that time is largely responsible for the inordinate amount of returns.

The Far Eastern Economic Review stated, "The Tokyo Stock Exchange is probably the most cynical, speculative, and manipulative stock market in the world.[28]"

Some people are afraid of market manipulation to the point that they believe it is impossible to overcome. Those individuals conclude that if markets are manipulated, then TA becomes worthless because big money traders can maneuver price to their benefit and anyone who trades against them is sure to learn a costly lesson.

Tyler argues that all markets are manipulated at all times, and the co-authors agree with this assertion. However, we also believe that it is possible to beat all markets through sound technical analysis and risk management.

If a market is being manipulated, then it will show up in the price and it will show up in the technicals.

The manipulative nature of the Japanese stock market is the primary reason why the hyperwave became so overinflated. Most return in the neighborhood of 800–2,000 percent. Bitcoin is the fastest-growing asset in human history, and even it was unable to exceed that threshold.

---

[28] Richards, B. (2017, May 23). *14 Fascinating Facts about Japanese Stocks—from 1989.* Retrieved from https://madison.com/business/investment/markets-and-stocks/fascinating-facts-about-japanese-stocks----from/article_af4fb635-e9a6-57fb-8822-d39cf5584ca1.html

Nevertheless, it was D. Tyler Jenks's most profitable investment, up to that point, and it was also his best call. Technical analysis is the reason why Tyler was able to make highly lucrative investments in a highly manipulated market.

This is another reason why we believe that technical analysis is so valuable. If implemented properly, it can protect investors and traders against market manipulation. If a person or group of people is manipulating the price, then it will show up in the technicals. If it does not show up in the technicals, then it means that the wannabe manipulators are not having any impact on price, despite their best efforts.

The trend is your friend regardless of the underlying cause. It does not matter if the price is increasing due to legitimate price discovery or manipulation. What matters is that the price is increasing; therefore, the trend is bullish.

Buying into a bull trend and exiting before it fully reverses is a key to trading and investing alike; however, it is much easier said than done. Hyperwave theory is perhaps the single most effective way to accomplish this goal. Buying into phase 3 ensures that one is trading with the trend, and selling as soon as a weekly candle closes below phase 4 ensures that one will exit before the trend fully reverses.

Following these rules allowed Tyler to sell another top shortly before the floor fell out. It also allowed him to be completely prepared for what was to follow. When the price was still over 30,000, he called for a return to the low four digits. Many would have argued that this is impossible due to fundamental reasons or trusting that the market manipulators would not allow this to occur.

Despite all the outside factors, Tyler understood the fate of the Japanese economy as a result of technical analysis. He also understood that the ensuing meltdown would only be exacerbated by the manipulation that had occurred, instead of believing that further manipulation would save the day. At the time, it was the best call of Tyler's career and the most money that he had ever made. This earned him a lot of respect and adoration among his colleagues and clients while also giving him tremendous confidence in his new theory.

Sugar

1970s Sugar Hyperwave

Sugar started to break out of phase 1 during the last few months of 1971, very shortly after President Nixon and Congress unilaterally terminated convertibility of the US dollar to gold.

In less than three years, the price of sugar had increased over 1,000 percent. This seems like a natural response to the world converting to fiat money. The money supply increased exponentially; therefore, so did the price in commodities. The world was forced to make the change as a result of the new policies in the US since most other developed countries were using US dollars to back their currencies (which was done under the presumption that US dollars were in turn backed by gold).

After 1971 there was no sound money safeguard that stopped the governments and central banks from printing as much as their hearts desired. As was discussed earlier in this book this proved to be an irresistible temptation for anyone who was given control of the printing press, and it marked the beginning of hyperinflation.

What followed is perhaps the most fascinating part of the story. When phase 4 of the hyperwave in sugar broke down, the price eventually returned to phase 1. More money continued to get injected into the system; however, the price of sugar fell back to pre-fiat prices. Price has remained very close to that level ever since. While the money supply has increased by over 3,000 percent since 1970, the price of sugar is barely up 100 percent. Sugar returned to phase 1 despite an ever-increasing supply of money.

This seems like quite the head-scratcher and is perhaps a result of price controls. The government has been subsidizing the sugar industry, as well as others, to combat the inflation that should have resulted from increasing the money supply. This keeps prices artificially low despite a very significant change in the monetary supply.

1970s Silver Hyperwave and 2000s Silver Funky Hyperwave

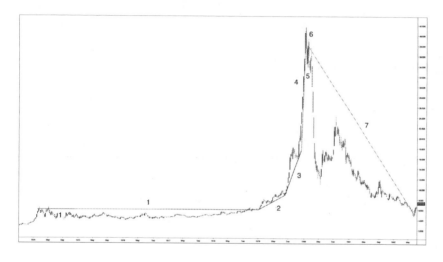

1970s Silver Hyperwave

The silver hyperwave that occurred in the late 1970s appears to be another direct result of Nixon closing the gold window. Now that the US dollar was no longer backed by gold or silver, the only way to redeem paper money for precious metals was to buy them from the free market.

Removing the last link to a gold standard meant that there was an influx of people who wanted to convert their paper money into physical gold or silver. The increase in demand caused commodities prices to skyrocket and silver increased by 680 percent over the following year.

Tyler completed his service in the coast guard in 1975 in Hawaii. His commanding officer had established a money management firm with Dean Witter and asked Tyler to join as soon as he finished serving.

He happily obliged and proceeded to start his career in finance with a splash by capitalizing on the run-up in silver. The rapidly increasing prices meant that jewelry and coins were often worth more than their face amount.

While the price was breaking out of phase 1, Tyler was going around Hawaii buying up all the silver he could get his hands on, from denizens (including numismatic coins) as well as financial institutions. He was willing to pay above face value because he already had it sold for a premium. Tyler made enough money buying and selling silver during the mid-1970s to buy his first condo.

That was only the tip of the iceberg.

This is right before the time that the Hunt brothers infamously tried to corner the silver market. They saw what Organization of the Petroleum Exporting Countries (OPEC) was doing with oil and figured that the same thing could be done with silver if they could get their hands on enough of it. At one point, the trio was estimated to hold one-third of the world's silver supply, excluding what was held by governments and central banks.

Tyler had a very high net worth client with direct ties to the Hunt Brothers. As the price rallying through $20, and then $30, this client was intent on increasing his exposure due to believing that the Hunt brothers would succeed in pushing the price into the triple-figure territory. Tyler did not share this opinion and implored the high roller to ease off the gas and instead start hedging by selling futures contracts. This advice was due to being acutely aware of what could happen if the carpet was pulled out from under the Hunts.

The walls in his office were covered with commodity charts during the time, and sugar was showing striking similarities to the silver market during 1980. They were so similar that Tyler got the two mixed up during a serendipitous phone call that took place with this high net worth client. While looking at the sugar chart, Tyler advised his client to start preparing for a reversal in silver.

After hanging up the phone, Tyler realized his mistake, but it did nothing to change his opinion about the advice he had just given his client. Both charts showed very similar technical setups with trend lines that were increasing so rapidly that they were almost at a ninety-degree angle. Tyler thought that this was an unsustainable move and all he had to do to grasp what could happen once the trend line broke down was look to the left of the sugar chart.

Sugar had been in a very similar posture five years prior, when it ran from $6 to over $60 and then back down to $6 in a matter of three years. This information reaffirmed Tyler's belief in the future of silver prices. He used this chart to enlighten his client about the risks of buying amid a vertical increase. Although there were multiple cooks in the kitchen, all of who had more experience than Tyler, the client heeded his advice and decided to proceed with caution.

Tyler got his clients out of the market right after the trend line broke down when the price was still in the mid $30s. This was about 15 percent from the peak and was only weeks before the price crashed over 50 percent in a month.

The Hunt brothers were highly overleveraged and eventually received a margin call that they were unable to cover. Shortly thereafter, the price began to tank and the consequences were wider reaching than most expected. They had borrowed so heavily that multiple large Wall Street banks and brokerage firms were at risk of collapsing. This caused the panic that is now known as Silver Thursday[29].

This experience led to the discovery of hyperwave patterns. The similarity between sugar and silver was too great to ignore, and Tyler used the repeating pattern to draw up the hyperwave archetype that hasn't changed to this day.

---

[29] Hurt III, H. (May 17, 1982) *Texas Rich: The Hunt Dynasty, From the Early Oil Days to the Silver Crash.* New York, NY: W.W. Norton & Company

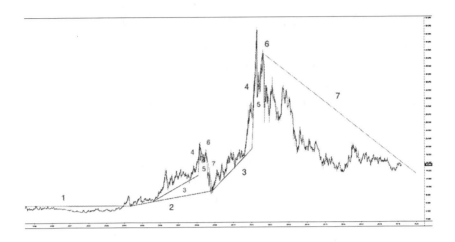

2000s Funky Hyperwave

Silver proceeded to create a funky hyperwave leading up to and following the 2008 mortgage crisis. It started to accelerate in 2009 after the first round of quantitative easing. This was very similar to what preempted the 1970s hyperwave—increasing the money supply resulted in commodities inflating accordingly.

It is hard to understand what happened next. The money supply continued to increase after 2012 while the price of silver and gold started going in the other direction. This is hard to explain from a fundamental point of view while being very important from a technical perspective.

Price proceeded to go down after closing below phase 4 in spite of extremely bullish fundamentals. This is a great example of how technicals tend to trump fundamentals.

General Electric Company

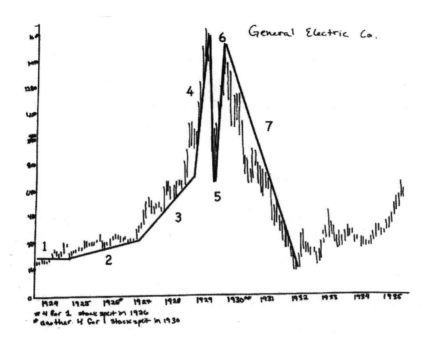

General Electric GE 1920s Hyperwave

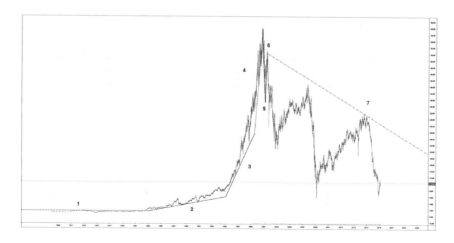

Second General Electric Company (NYSE: GE) Hyperwave

General Electric has experienced two hyperwaves over the past century. The first one occurred in the 1920s and 1930s, and it was the single most perfected hyperwave that we have found. The apexes, duration, and amplitude of each phase are ideal. It did everything that it was supposed to do right when it was supposed to do it. The one thing to note is that this is a monthly chart. We have searched for a weekly GE chart from that time period and have come up empty. When the monthly is this perfected, it is hard to think that the weekly would differ significantly. Nevertheless, it would be very nice to verify that assumption. Even without the necessary data, we are still comfortable concluding that this is the single best hyperwave that has ever occurred.

GE established another hyperwave in the 1980s that is still active in 2019. While the first was the most textbook hyperwave we can find, the one that followed is one of the most maniacal phase 7's that we have seen. The crash from 2007 to 2009 broke down phase 2, and it was very close to returning to phase 1. However, it found support, out of nowhere, and price proceeded to rally 500 percent before creating a third lower high. It then gave up all those gains in very short order, fully retracing in less than two years. Yet again it appears to have found support before returning to phase 1.

Phase 7 has lasted close to twenty years, which is already longer than phases 2, 3, and 4 combined. The only other example we have of such a lengthy phase 7 is from the hyperwave that occurred in interest rates following the closure of the gold window. That phase 7 lasted for twenty-two years.

Keep in mind that phase 7 in GE will remain intact until price creates a new ATH or closes below the phase 1 trend line. If price gets another strong bounce from horizontal support, then it could take another decade, or more, for that to happen. As it stands right now, this is expected to be the longest phase 7 that has ever occurred.

It is very important to keep this in mind while looking at the other major hyperwaves that are currently active. The longer the bull phases last, the longer phase 7 is expected to be. If a hyperwave spends more than twenty-five years in phases 2, 3, and 4, then the reaction in phase 7 is expected to be very lengthy as well.

The following are the cumulative length of the second, third, and fourth phases of currently active hyperwaves:

- S&P 500: 37 years
- Boeing: 37 years
- Dow Jones Industrial Average: 35 years
- McDonald's: 35 years
- Nasdaq 100: 28 years
- Value line Index: 27 years

CHAPTER 21

LIMITATIONS OF HYPERWAVES

Shortest active hyperwave: Bitcoin

- active for 5 years, 2 months, 24 days

Shortest completed hyperwave: 1974–1982 Silver

- active for 8 years, 3 months, 13 days

Longest completed hyperwave: 30-Year US Treasury yield

- active for 42 years

Longest completed funky hyperwave: Dow Chemicals, which later became DowDupont

- active for 100 years

Longest active hyperwave: S&P 500

- active for 37 years
- only in phase 3!

Smallest amplitude: Bethlehem Steel

- returned 290% from phase 1

Largest amplitude: Nikkei 225

- returned 4,00% from phase 1

The above limitations allow us to better understand the price movement and time aspect; however it does not make any such predictions. It simply helps us to understand that there is a very high probability of hyperwaves honoring these limitations.

This is important for a variety of reasons and is primarily why we are so hesitant to label Ethereum as a hyperwave. It returned 100X from the start of phase 2 to the peak of phase 4, and it did so in record speed.

If we consider Ethereum a hyperwave, then we would have to admit that it is the shortest ever in terms of time while it has the largest percentage return, more than doubling second place. It does appear to be crystalizing like a snowflake; however, those two factors make it extremely different from all the other snowflakes, even though the structure appears to be the same.

We are not saying that it is impossible to break the limitations that have been observed; however, we are saying that it is a cause to be very suspicious, especially when the limitations are violated so significantly. The fact that it is larger and traveling at a much faster velocity makes it seem more similar to hail than snow.

PHASE 6

COMPLEMENTING HYPERWAVE THEORY

CHAPTER 22

DEVELOPING A HIERARCHY OF INDICATORS

Identifying hyperwaves in hindsight is quite simple relative to trading or investing in them in real time. Phases are often dubious in real time while being crystal clear in hindsight. When price starts to accelerate from a phase line, it can be very difficult to know if it is starting the next phase or if it is simply getting overextended from the current phase. When that happens, the best opportunities can be left in the rearview mirror.

Unfortunately, this is a lesson that can only be learned the hard way.

There will be times when you enter a long right before the price plummets. There will be times when the price proceeds to skyrocket shortly after taking out your stop-loss. There will be times when the phase line is drawn incorrectly. There will be times when you get overexposed, which is likely to lead to mismanaging the stop-loss and take profit orders. Fifteen percent of patterns break down in phase 3 without ever entering the fourth and most lucrative phase.

The only way to learn how to beat the market is to make every mistake under the sun while remaining solvent and resilient. As the old saying goes, "If it was easy, then everyone would do it."

After developing a strong understanding of how to identify a hyperwave, most will want to learn how to trade or invest in them. The best way is to buy phase 3 and exit after a weekly close below phase 4. A more advanced approach entails short selling phase 6 or 7 after taking profit at the beginning of phase 5. That is much easier said than done; therefore, it can be very beneficial to complement hyperwaves with other reliable indicators and patterns.

Consensio

Consensio is the second most powerful indicator of our hierarchy. It would be number 1 if there weren't so many active hyperwaves. Tyler developed it to trade numismatic coins, but it can be implemented in all markets, at all times.

It uses moving averages to identify the trend as well as to signal entries and exits. The subconditions are designed to enter a position before a bull trend and take full profit before it fully reverses. Following the rules outlined in *Deep Dive into Consensio*[30] mathematically guarantees that one will not miss out on a trend.

If following Consensio, then one will be fully entered into an asset long before it enters phase 3. It will signal an entry shortly after the asset breaks out of phase 1. However, if those signals were missed because the hyperwave was found after the fact, then it can still be used to time entries when the asset tests phase 3 or falls below it.

Moving averages or exponential moving averages can be used depending on the users' preference. The creator of the system uses the former while the coauthor prefers the latter.

We also tend to use slightly different periods, and that is okay. Everyone should make slight adjustments, and that is primarily a function of volatility and time frame. In faster markets, shorter-term moving averages are preferred. When using smaller time frames, such as the daily or the 4h, then longer-term MA's are preferred. The default periods are 2, 7, and 30 on the Weekly timeframe.

---

[30] Jenks, D.T. & Wald, L. [Hyperwave]. (2018, June 21). *Deep Dive Into Consensio*. Retrieved from https://www.youtube.com/watch?v=xwW8h0lrQ-I&frags=pl%2Cwn

What is important is that the price stays above the short-term MA when in a strong trend. Minor corrections should find support at the medium-term MA, and major corrections should find support from the long-term MA.

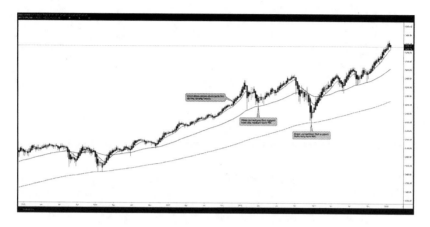

S&P 500 Consensio

Reversals are signaled when price fails to support the long-term MA and confirmation comes when the long-term MA rolls over. The angle of the long-term moving average determines the trend. When it is angled up, the trend is bullish. When it is angled down, the trend is bearish. When it turns over after a prolonged trend, then it signals a reversal.

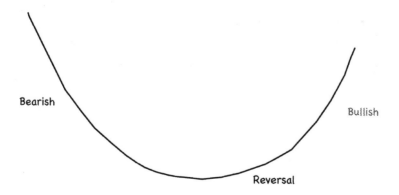

Consensio

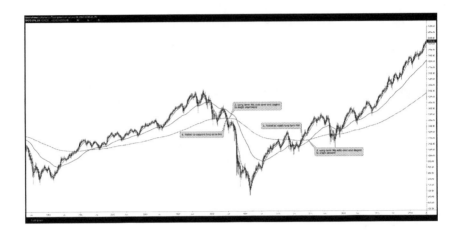

S&P 500 Consensio Reversal

Exits are signaled when the price falls below the long-term MA as well as when the medium- and short-term MA's make bearish crossovers. Bearish crossovers happen when the short-term MA's cross below the long-term MA. Bullish crossovers signal entries and occur when short-term cross above the long-term.

If one is using Consensio to time long entries in phase 3, then the bullish crossovers will have already occurred and a different set of rules will be used. A percentage of the position can be entered when price tests the medium-term MA, and another portion is saved for the long-term MA.

As long as the long-term MA is angled up, then the trend is bullish and that area should be very strong support.

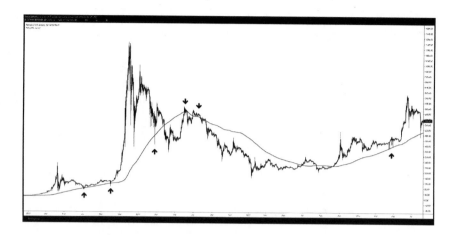

Consensio Long-Term MA Support

Notice how the 200 day MA acted as support for Bitcoin as long as it was trending up. It quickly because resistance after rolling over. That is impressive, but will always lag Hyperwave. When the asset is in a hyperwave it will get very extended from the moving averages. As a result using them to time exits will not be preferred when the asset is in a hyperwave. If it is progressing in a more linear fashion then MA's and Consensio will be an excellent way to time exits as well as entries.

This is a prime example of why we place hyperwave at the top of the totem pole.

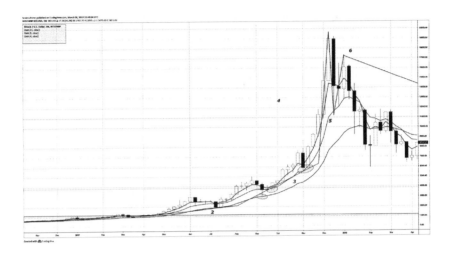

Consensio Applied to Bitcoin in Phase 3

In this case, price only tested the long-term (exponential) moving average one time during phase 3. And it happened so early on that it would have been impossible to know that phase 3 was beginning. The medium-term (exponential) moving average was only tested twice thereafter, and both were during phase 3 retests.

With X position size, the aggressive approach would be to enter 25–50 percent at the medium-term MA and the remainder can be entered on long-term MA retests. The more conservative approach would save 33–50 percent for confirmation from a weekly close above the phase line. In this case, the long-term MA is below the phase line, and testing that area for support means that the phase line is in danger of breaking down. Therefore, it is more conservative to wait for the weekly candle to close above the phase line relative to entering orders at/near the MA.

Seeing a bullish moving average in confluence with a phase line provides very powerful confirmation of the entry point. Saving a percentage of the investment for a test of the long-term moving average will sometimes mean that only a portion of the position gets entered. In that case, it is a good idea to have a backup plan, such as adding if / when a new high is reached.

Gaps in Price

As we learned in the introduction to technical analysis, prior resistance is expected to become support following a breakthrough. This is by far the most common way for price to progress, especially in linear markets. It starts with two steps forward, one through resistance and another to form a higher high. That is followed with one step back to retest prior resistance for support. From there it is primed to take another two steps forward, so on and so forth. This doesn't always happen, and it can provide a very powerful indication when trading hyperwaves.

When price breaks through a horizontal boundary line, then a throwback is expected to retest that area for support. Sometimes it will not hold as support and the price will proceed to retrace back into the middle of the trading range. This is known as a bull trap.

On the other end of the spectrum, what happens when the price fails to return to the prior resistance line? Sometimes the price will continue to rally strong and the following correction will find support well above the old boundary line. This is known as a gap in price.

When gaps do not get filled, it is likely because the price is respecting a phase line that is too steep to allow for a return to prior horizontal resistance.

Gaps in Price on the Turkish Lira

A very important rule of thumb to remember is that horizontal support and resistance is always more important than trend lines are, *unless the asset is in a hyperwave.*

Phase lines are so powerful that they move up the technical analysis totem pole and supersede horizontals. This is not true in any other trading environment. Remember that all phase lines are trend lines but very few trend lines are phase lines. Trend lines occur in all market structures, whereas phase lines only occur in hyperwaves.

Phase lines > Horizontals > Trend Lines

This can be very useful when trying to identify hyperwaves in real time. After noticing a gap in price that does not get filled, it can be a good opportunity to enter. This occurs due to the demand drastically outweighing the supply and the front running that will follow.

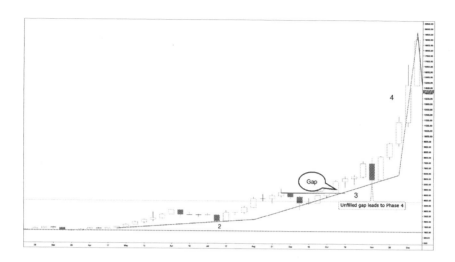

Bitcoin Gap in Price before Phase 4

The Bitcoin hyperwave in 2017 is a great example of this principle. The price struggled to break through $5,000 for six weeks during the autumn, and once it did, the hyperwave started to establish itself.

Traders who missed the opportunity to buy that breakout set their sights on buying big when the price returned to retest prior resistance for support. Many were expecting another large move to follow and didn't care if they entered right at the expected area of support or if it was a small percentage above.

If expecting the price to rally to at least $7,500 after supporting a throwback, then it is a common phenomenon for people to focus on getting filled instead of getting the best price. Getting filled at $5,100 was more important than risking missing out and trying to get the best price at approximately $5,000.

This perpetuates and others will enter orders at $5,150 and $5,200. This is considered frontrunning, and it will often result in the price finding support before returning to old resistance. When this happens, it is a very strong sign of an exuberant marketplace. This could be thought of as a change in sentiment, which is a necessity for establishing a new phase. Failing to throw back to prior resistance leaves an unfilled gap, and that is a strong indication that the next phase is attempting to establish itself.

One of the most difficult parts of trading hyperwaves in real time is distinguishing between when the price is overextended from the current phase and when a new phase is beginning. The ability to consistently recognize the start of a new phase allows one to find some great entries. Conversely, if new phases are not properly labeled, then it could result in unfavorable entries with suboptimal stop-losses.

The Turkish lira is a prime example. The run-up in September and August could easily be labeled phase 4, and the move that followed looked very much like a 5, 6, and 7.

Turkish Lira if in Phase 7

This is how we were drawing the hyperwave during the fall and winter of 2018. However, the sell-off appears to be finding support before retesting prior horizontal resistance at $4.95. This provided a strong indication that it was still in phase 3 and that the move in August was not a phase 4; instead it was simply an overextension from phase 3.

It was time to reevaluate after seeing the support at $5.18 along with the gap in price between there and $4.95. Further analysis indicated that the phase 3 needed to be adjusted.

Unfilled Gaps in the Turkish Lira

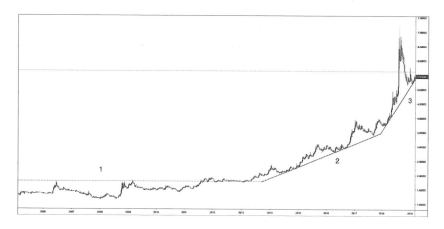

Dollar Turkish Lira | USDTRY Hyperwave if in Phase 3

If the new phase 3 holds, then it would imply that phase 4 has yet to happen, which would suggest that this is a great buying opportunity. This would have been almost impossible to recognize in real time without the unfilled gap.

This is a great example of how to complement hyperwave with other tools to properly recognize phases in real time. It is certainly possible that characterizing USDTRY as phase 3 turns out to be incorrect; however, this remains the most probable phase as long as the gap remains unfilled.

Phase Channels

Another reliable way to recognize new phases is through parallel channels. Parallel channels that occur with phase lines are referred to as phase channels. When price breaks through the top of a parallel channel, then it is a strong indication that the next phase is beginning.

This is an area where traps are likely to occur, so it is best to proceed with caution and wait for a supported throwback or further confirmation before being confident in the next phase beginning.

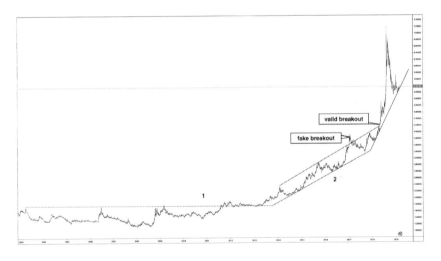

Turkish Lira Phase Channel with Fake Breakout Followed by Valid Breakout

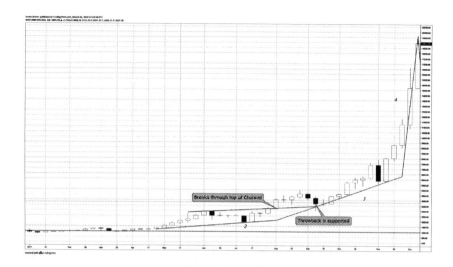

**Bitcoin Breaks through Phase 2 Channel and Supports
Throwback before Establishing Phase 3**

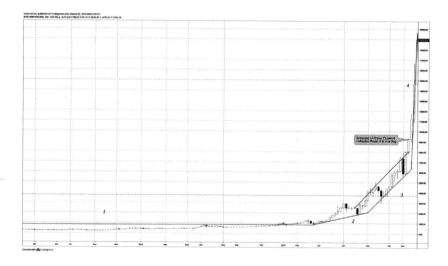

Bitcoin Breaks through Phase 3 Channel and Enters Phase 4 without a Pullback

The price won't always retest the top of the channel, and that is especially common when entering phase 4. If that happens and the market leaves us behind then we have to be okay with kissing it goodbye. There will always be another train coming and it is often how we respond to the missed entries that matters more than how we respond to the perfect setups.

Nasdaq Phase 3 Channel Following Weekly Candle Close on March 1, 2019

At the time of writing, the US equity markets remain in a very interesting intersection. The question that we have been trying to answer is if phase 4 already occurred from January 2, 2017, to August 1, 2018, or if that was still phase 3.

Since the pullback at the end of 2018 found support from the top of the phase 3 channel, without refilling the gap from April 24, 2017, we are inclined to think that phase 4 has not yet started. If we are right, then we should expect to see the Nasdaq 100 over 15,000 within the next 3 -5 years, and that would likely put the S&P 500 in the 6,000 neighborhood.

If we are wrong, then phase 4 broke down on October 25, 2018, and the 20 percent rally that kicked off 2019 was nothing more than a phase 5 move. Since we know that phase 5 cannot exceed phase 4's all-time high, we know exactly what to watch for from here.

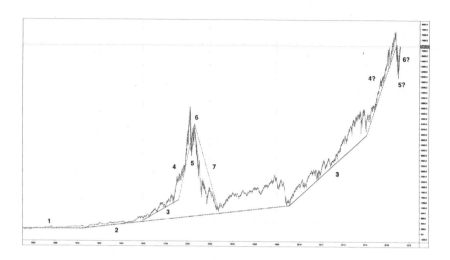

Nasdaq Funky Hyperwave if Using January 2, 2017, to August 1, 2018, as Phase 4

This is very similar to USDTRY in that it would be possible to argue that phase 4 has yet to happen and there are also many reasons to argue we are in phase 6 which implies that the upside is finished.

Seeing the unfilled gap in price along with the support from the top of the phase channel provides strong evidence that phase 4 still has not occurred. However, it is still too soon to be overly confident in either direction. If the current rally takes out the prior all-time high, then we can be very confident that this was only phase 3. If the low that is marked phase 5 above gets taken out, then we can be very confident that phases 4, 5, and 6 ran their course and now it has entered phase 7.

During times of uncertainty, it is crucial to know when and how to reach deeper into the toolbox in an attempt to peak through the fog.

Coppock Curve

The Coppock curve was introduced by Edwin Sedgwick in 1962 in a short article featured in *Barron's* magazine. It is calculated as a ten-month weighted moving average using the sum of the fourteen-month rate of change and the eleven-month rate of change.

This oscillator has an uncanny ability to call market tops and bottoms. As the calculation would suggest, it is best used on the monthly chart. When it crosses above 0, that is indicative of a bottom and when it falls below 0, that is indicative of a top.

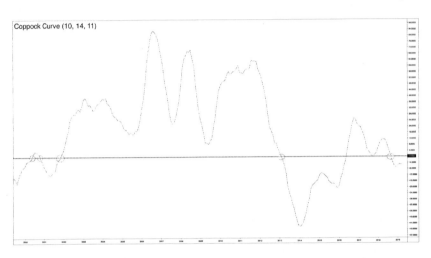

Coppock Curve on Gold, 1999–2019

Signals are extremely rare; in the case of gold, it only crossed the zero thresholds five times in twenty years. We believe that rarer signals are more valuable and reliable. The Coppock curve is a great example of this principle.

It was originally designed to call bottoms, opposed to tops, but we believe it is equally as effective in both areas.

This can be especially useful in a muddled environment, such as what we are currently experiencing in the Nasdaq 100. If it is in phase 6, then we would expect the Coppock to be crossing below 0 or getting very close to it. If this is still phase 3, then we would expect the Coppock to be well above 0.

In these types of situations, the Coppock curve carries a lot of weight.

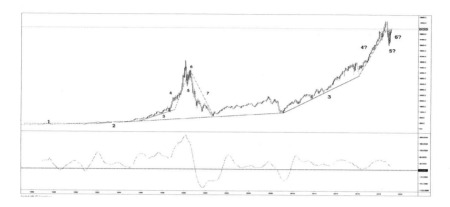

Nasdaq 100 Coppock Curve

The Coppock is expected to provide a sell signal in the vicinity of phase 6, or at the beginning of phase 7, and it is currently postured to do just that. If the index fails to make a new all-time high in 2019, then the sell signal appears imminent and it would provide a strong confirmation of where we stand in the hyperwave pattern.

On the other side of the coin, one might argue that we have not entered phase 4 as of yet because the Coppock curve has stayed below 80. That person could point to the amplitude of the oscillator in 2000 and use that as an indication that 2016–2019 was just a phase 3 that was overextended from the trend line, which is a common occurrence.

It remains too early to be overly confident one way or the other. If the Coppock crosses below 0, then it could be wise to exit long exposure, or at least look for hedging opportunities, regardless of how one is inclined to draw the hyperwave.

Average Directional Index (ADX)

The average directional index was originally developed by Welles Wilder in the 1960s for daily commodity charts; however, it can be used across all asset classes and all time frames. When this indicator was created, the idea was to separate buying and selling pressure from price.

It is not an oscillator, even though it has a similar appearance. When you get a top or a bottom, it is not a buy or a sell signal. The way the ADX works is when you get a bottom or a top, this an indication of a trend becoming exhausted. This is expected to precede a reversal but not necessarily in the direction the ADX is changing.

Many people who use the ADX will draw a horizontal line at 25 and will disregard tops that occur below that level. We like to see tops above 30 and bottoms below 20.

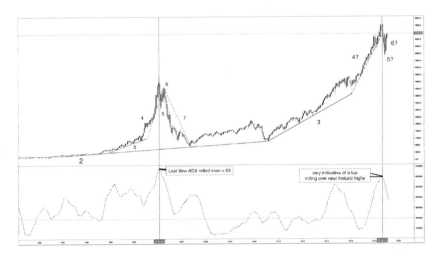

Average Directional Index (ADX) Applied to Monthly Nasdaq 100 Chart

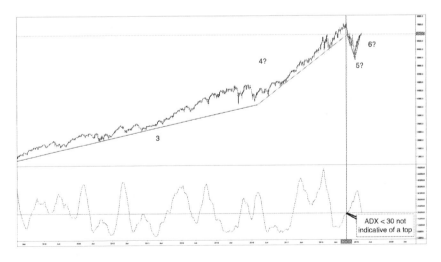

Average Directional Index Applied to Weekly Nasdaq 100 Chart

In this situation, it looks like the ADX is as confused as we are. The monthly is showing strong signs of a top, and the weekly begs to disagree. A very important rule of thumb is that the longer the time frame, the more weight it carries. In this circumstance, we are much more likely to believe the monthly chart.

Hierarchy of Indicators

When getting mixed signals, it is very important to understand how much weight to give to each indicator. We know that high time frames carry more weight than shorter time frames, but what about different indicators being used on the same time frame?

This is when it is crucial to understand where each indicator fits into the hierarchy. It is also very important to know when to move one up or down the totem pole. Hyperwaves are very rare and unique; therefore, very particular adjustments to the pecking order are required.

Different tools are needed for different jobs. Some tools that are very useful for one task could be completely disregarded while working on a different task. It doesn't necessarily mean one provides more utility than the other. It simply means that the individual must know when, where, and how to adjust what is carried in his or her toolbelt.

Some of our favorite tools become irrelevant while in phase 3 or phase 4 of a hyperwave. The relative strength index and stochastic oscillator are two very useful indicators; however, they are almost rendered useless when the market is in a hyperwave. Knowing when to remove those from the toolbelt and what to replace them with is key.

Hyperwave Hierarchy

- Phase lines
- Consensio
- Unfilled gaps
- Phase channels
- Coppock curve
- ADX

A weekly close below a phase line is the single most important indicator in a hyper-wave—by a long shot. When the pattern is clear as day in real time, then nothing else is needed.

Most hyperwaves will look picture-perfect in hindsight, but that is not usually the case in real time. This is why it is important to come equipped with more than one arrow in the quiver.

The second most important indicator is Consensio, specifically the angle of the long-term moving average. As long as it is angled up, the trend is bullish; when it is angled down, the trend is bearish. This can help us to distinguish phases when it is unclear if the asset is in phase 3 or has already entered phase 5, 6, or 7.

If the price is finding support above a bullish long-term moving average, then it is highly likely to still be in phase 3. If the long-term MA is rolling over and the price is breaking down below it, then that provides a strong indication that the asset is phase 7. Consensio can also be used to time or confirm entries. When a bullish MA is in confluence with the phase line, then that confirms it is an area of support.

Next on the list is looking for unfilled gaps in the price. When price action leaves unfilled gaps that are strongly indicative of front running and/or a phase line taking control.

This is also a strong sign that a market is advancing in a parabolic fashion. Linear markets will almost always retest prior resistance for support and fill the gaps in price. When a market consistently leaves unfilled gaps, then it will progress in a nonlinear fashion, which could form a parabola, blow-off top, or a hyperwave.

Horizontals are always more important than trend lines except when a market is going parabolic. When a market is in a parabola, or hyperwave it will consistently ignore the horizontals in favor of a curved or angular trendline.

When angular phase lines overpower horizontals, then the price will not be allowed to return to prior horizontal resistance to test it for support. Instead, it will find support above that area. When that happens we will look to plot a best fit trendline.

When the best fit areas of support are accelerating trendlines then the market is very likely to be in a hyperwave. When the best fit area of support is a curved trendline then the market is very likely to be in the midst of a parabola.

Remember that all hyperwaves are bubbles but not all bubbles are hyperwaves.

Phase channels, Coppock curve, and the average directional index round out the top six most important indicators to use to complement hyperwave theory. Breaking through the top of a phase channel suggests that the next phase is starting to establish itself. Coppock curve crossing below 0, on the monthly chart, indicates or confirms that phase 4 is over and phases 5, 6, and 7 are taking over. The average directional index helps to identify tops when the ADX rolls over after a prolonged trend.

CHAPTER 23

APPLYING HIERARCHY
IN REAL TIME

By putting it all together, hopefully we can develop a picture with a higher resolution. The Nasdaq 100 is showing a lot of mixed signals from some very powerful indicators, and it provides a great opportunity to apply the hierarchy in real time.

Starting from the top of the list, let's analyze Consensio using the fifty-week EMA as our long-term exponential moving average.

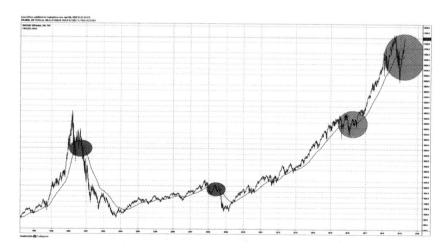

**Consensio Applied to the Nasdaq 100 Using the Fifty
EMA as the Long-Term Moving Average**

The red circles highlight areas when the long-term moving average changed directions, or rolled over, after a prolonged bull trend. As long as it was trending up, it acted as support. In 2000 it rolled over right as it was entering the seventh phase. In 2008, it rolled over right before the meltdown of subprime mortgages.

In 2016 it tried to roll over but held strong. Shortly after it started flattening out, the price rallied to new all-time highs. This prompt caused the moving average to resume its bullish trend. It appears as though something similar is currently happening. The sell-off at the end of 2018 broke down the long-term moving average and continued to sell off for the week. This caused the MA to flatten. While it was starting to roll over, the price shot back through and the MA resumed its bullish trend shortly thereafter.

These oscillations can occur prior to a reversal, and during times like this, it is prudent to proceed with caution. If the price fails to create a new all-time high, then the long-term moving average will be in danger of rolling over yet again. Notice how that would be similar to what happened in 2008 before the crash.

Another comparison that we can make is the distance from the fifty-week EMA during phase 3 and phase 4 that occurred in 2000.

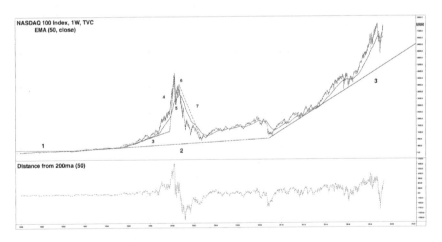

Nasdaq 100 Distance from 50 EMA

Notice how close the price stayed to the fifty-week EMA during the 2016–2018 run-up. That is cognizant of phase 3. Notice the price action from 1995 to 1998. While in phase 3, the price continually tested the fifty-week EMA. After entering phase 4, the price became overextended from the moving average. This can be confirmed with an indicator on trading view labeled "Distance from 200 MA." This can be adjusted in the settings to fifty, and it is the blue oscillator below the chart. Notice the enormous spike during phase 4 compared to the current environment. We are currently close to the average distance away from the moving average, which is something we would expect in phases 1–3 but not in phase 4, 5, 6, or 7.

When price runs away from its longer-term moving averages, then that is highly unsustainable and likely to be met with an equal and opposite reaction. Both are a hallmark of phases 4–7, and the distance from the MA provide strong confirmation that we have yet to enter the fourth phase.

All in all, Consensio is looking bullish; however, it is far from being out of the woods just yet.

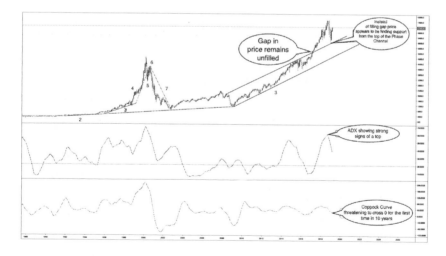

Hierarchy of Indicators Applied to the Nasdaq 100

Moving down the list, we can start looking for gaps in price. Gaps are most likely to occur after a major boundary line is violated. This could be horizontal resistance or the top of a phase channel.

As we can see above, there is a massive unfilled gap that occurred toward the end of 2017. Instead of filling the gap, price appears to be finding support from the top of the phase channel. Both are very strong indications that it is still trying to establish phase 4 and that the recent sell-off was a correction opposed to a reversal.

Moving down the list, we see the Coppock curve threatening to cross below 0 while the average directional index is showing strong signs of a top. Without understanding where each indicator falls on the hierarchy, it would be nearly impossible to decipher the mixed signals.

After understanding the importance of each, we can weigh the various signals accordingly.

Consensio > Unfilled Gaps > Phase Channel Breakthrough > Coppock Curve > Average Directional Index

As long as the price fails to fill in gaps that were left from violating major areas of resistance, we are inclined to expect phase 4 to eventually establish itself. This would indicate that the price is supporting the next leg up in the bull market.

We can paint a clearer picture after applying the hierarchy of indicators but that does not necessarily imply that it is time to take a position. This is a prime example of when it would be a good idea to wait for further confirmation to enter or look for hedging/profit-taking opportunities to protect long exposure that is well into the green.

If the price retraces back into the phase 3 channel, then it will almost certainly fill the gap in price, and that would likely be in confluence with the Coppock crossing 0. When everything is lining up and painting the same picture, then it is usually a great opportunity to take a position. Until then, cash is king!

If the price creates a new all-time high, then that confirms we are still in phase 3 and/or on the verge of starting phase 4. We know that phase 6 does not create a new high above phase 4's peak; therefore, it is a very good final confirmation to wait for.

This is a good example of how to prepare for price movement in either direction when the picture is muddled. Having the patience and discipline to wait for confirmation while trading or investing in murky markets is one of the most important keys to long-term success.

CHAPTER 24

Two Patterns That Complement Hyperwave

The indicators provided above will help one to identify and confirm different phases of a hyperwave. This section will cover two patterns that can occur inside hyperwaves which can provide great opportunities to enter. We will also go over an example that illustrates how to manage risk by capitalizing on partial profits.

The Cup and Handle

"The Cup and Handle" chart pattern was defined by William O'Neil in the book *How to Make Money in Stocks,* which was published in 1988. The nomenclature is very appropriate. The only difference between this pattern and an actual coffee cup is that the handle should be situated in the top quadrant of the cup. If the handle retraces too far, then it invalidates the pattern.

A cup and handle, often abbreviated to C&H, is a bullish continuation pattern and is very well suited for timing entries in phase 3 of a hyperwave. An entry is triggered when price breaks through horizontal resistance, which represents the brim of the cup and the top of the handle.

Once confirmed, a cup and handle has a 62 percent chance of reaching its target[31]. The target is measured by adding the depth of the cup to the top of the brim.

---

[31] Bulkowski, T. *Bulkowski's Cup with Handle.* Retrieved from http://thepatternsite.com/cup.html

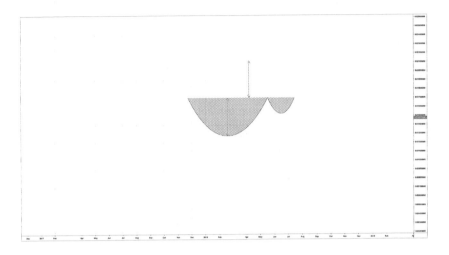

Measuring Price Target Using Cup and Handle

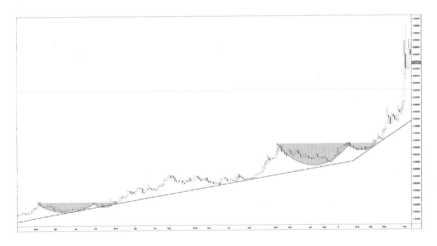

Turkish Lira Cup and Handles

The Turkish lira formed two brilliant cup and handles in 2014 and 2017. Both provided excellent entries into a hyperwave. We see that both reach their respective price targets in a relatively short amount of time and then continued to rally right on through.

If looking for entries into phase 3 of a hyperwave, then using patterns such as cup and handles are a high probability and relatively low-risk way to do so. In this case, the profit target from the pattern can either be completely disregarded or used as an area to *trim* the position. Phase 4 of the hyperwave is the target; the C&H is simply being used to time entries.

Trimming can also be referred to as *taking partial profit,* and this is a very good way to manage risk. If entering X upon the cup and handle confirmation, then a great approach would be to take partial profit, in the neighborhood of 1/5–1/3X, after reaching the measured move from the C&H. This is a way to guarantee the position is profitable, even if it is one of the 15 percent of hyperwaves that never enter into phase 4. This approach also maintains a healthy amount of exposure based on the expectation that phase 4 is around the corner.

That may be confusing, so let us run through a quick example because it is a very important concept.

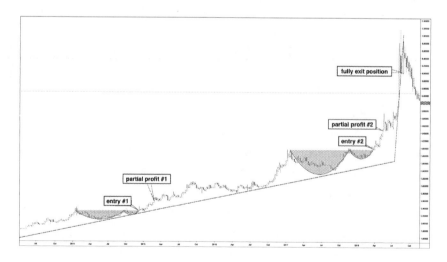

USD TRY | Dollar Turkish Lira Practice Trade

- In this example, let's assume that X = $10,000.
- A long position is entered on December 14, 2016, as soon as the C&H pattern is confirmed.
- Price = $2.313.
- Profit target = $2.5402.

- Decide to trim 25 percent of position if C&H profit target is reached.
- C&H target is reached on March 2, 2015. The position is +9.81 percent; therefore, our $2,500 is now $2,745.
- At this point, it would be a very good idea to move the stop-loss up to breakeven. Doing so guarantees that the position will be profitable; the minimum profit would be +$245, or +2.45%, less any fees.
- This allows us to hold onto a healthy amount of exposure in anticipation of phase 4 being around the corner, and we can do so without assuming any risk (outside of exchange risk, which is the small chance that an exchange goes insolvent while the position is still open).
- At the beginning of 2018, we notice the phase 3 holding strong and another cup and handle forming. At this point, the original position is deep into profit, and this is an opportunity to increase exposure. Using the same approach, we can enter another $10,000 with a plan to trim at the profit target of $4.46.
- Entry is executed on March 22, 2018, as soon as the pattern is confirmed. The price for the second entry is $3.99.
- On May 11, 2018, the price reaches the C&H target at $4.46. Again we trim 25 percent of the new position and get $2,794.25 returned to the trading account. We then move the stop-loss to break even and ensure a little bit of profit in the event that phase 3 breaks down.
- At this point, we have $15,000 in exposure and $539.25 in realized profit.
- Now we can plan on holding onto the full $15,000 in exposure with an expectation of phase 4 being around the corner and plan to take full profit when the weekly candle closes below phase 3 or phase 4.
- Asset appears to enter phase 4 in August 2018 after breaking through $5.00.
  - This is the hardest phase line to draw due to how steep of an angle it is and the lack of pullbacks. In this case, we draw a nearly vertical line using the weekly opens.
- Weekly candle closes below phase 4 on August 20, 2018, and full profit is taken at $5.995.
- The average price on our $15,000 in exposure = $3.06.
  - $2.1313 + $3.99/2 = $3.06.
- The return on the remainder of our investment = +95.91 percent.
  - $5.995 (exit) - $3.06 (enter) = $2.935.
  - $2.935/$3.06 = 0.9591 (ROI).

- $15,000 (exposure) * 1.9591 (ROI) = $29,386 (total amount returned).
- $29,386 (total returned) - $15,000 (cost) = +$14,386 (net profit).
- $14,386 (net profit) + $539.25 (previously realized profit) = $14,925.75 (total net profit).

The example above outlines a real-world scenario where someone could return approximately 100 percent in less than four years using hyperwave and a complementary pattern to time entries and manage risk. Trimming is a very powerful approach to protect unrealized profits. Finding patterns that occur amid a hyperwave is a very reliable way to do so.

Ascending Triangles

An ascending triangle is characterized by higher lows and a horizontal resistance line at the top. The pattern should be created with at least five touch points and is confirmed when price breaks through the horizontal boundary. Some will wait for a close to confirm the breakout, while others are willing to enter as soon as price violates resistance.

The profit target is calculated by measuring the length between the first two touch points (points 1 and 2 in the example below) and extending that from the horizontal resistance line. When ascending triangles break out to the upside, they have a 75 percent likelihood of reaching the measured move[32].

Ascending triangles complement hyperwaves quite nicely because they will usually be a phase line that provides the support that leads to the higher lows. The strategy is the same as it would be for cup and handles.

Wait for confirmation to provide a high probability and low-risk entry. Trim 20–33 percent of the position at the price target that is provided from the complementary pattern, then don't be afraid to rinse and repeat if similar patterns appear later in the move.

---

[32] Bulkowski, T. *Bulkowski's Ascending Triangles*. Retrieved from http://thepatternsite.com/at.html

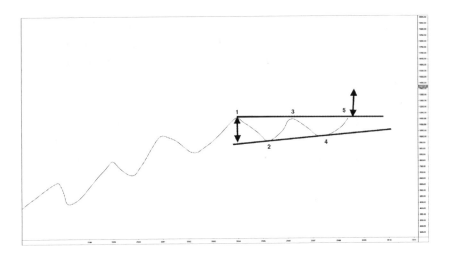

Texas Instruments Ascending Triangle

Following the crash in 2008 and 2009, Texas Instruments began to establish a funky hyperwave. After finding support at the phase 2 trend line, the second phase 3 started to take shape. Two higher lows were formed in August 2015 and January 2016.

That allows phase 3 to be drawn in, and it also created an ascending triangle in the process. Price broke through the upside after the fifth touch point, and that provided a great opportunity to enter around $60.

The distance between point 1 ($60) and point 2 ($45) is $15; therefore, the target for trimming is $75 ($60 + $15). Since this is a hyperwave, we would prefer to hold the majority of the position through that area. If this was an ascending triangle that is not a part of a hyperwave, then full profit would be taken upon reaching the target.

The fact that the asset is in a confirmed hyperwave is the most important variable, and ancillary patterns are simply used to time entries into phase 3 as well as to manage risk by trimming once the price reaches the measured move.

A confirmed phase 3 is the best time to look for long exposure. It will offer the highest probabilities, the most asymmetric risk: reward and an extremely favorable time horizon relative to the potential return on investment. The most important factors to consider when making any trade are the following:

- risk versus reward
- probability of taking a loss
- chances of hitting the target
- chances of capitalizing on a profit but not reaching the target
- how long it takes for the trade to develop

All ROI's are not created equally. Let's consider two people who are touting a 100 percent return on investment.

Person A

- wasn't using a stop-loss and therefore was putting 100 percent of the position at risk
- did not consider or calculate the probability of taking a loss
- took ten years to achieve the 100 percent ROI
- ROI is on paper

Person B

- set stop-loss 20 percent below entry price and was not willing to assume more risk under any circumstances
- had a clear understanding of the strike rate, knowing that 85 percent of the time the trade is expected to return a profit while understooding that the stop-loss would be executed the other 15 percent of the time
- implemented a trailing stop-loss system to protect unrealized profit, which helps to ensure small profits even if the profit target is never reached
- took ten months to achieve the 100 percent ROI
- ROI is fully realized

Person A represents the typical buy and holder. Individuals who buy and hold investments will usually not have a set stop-loss, which means all their money is at risk. That person also does not understand the success rate that can be expected.

Most will assume that if they can hold onto the investment for long enough, then it is essentially guaranteed to turn a profit. This strategy could easily net a 100 percent ROI in a ten-year bull market, but they will not know when, how, or if to capitalize on the profit. Therefore, person A could think that they have returned 100 percent ROI, but they are sorely mistaken if that return is on paper instead of being realized.

Anyone who has held onto an investment through a major correction, or bear market, understands that returns on paper can, and will, evaporate much more quickly than they materialized.

Person B understands that consistently beating the market starts and ends with risk management. Moving from cash into a speculative investment or trade is extremely risky, even with a stop-loss, and without the ability to properly manage risk, it is impossible to consistently beat the market over the long run. Person B understands this concept all too well and has learned to limit exposure to risk through the implementation of stop-losses.

If the position moves in that person's favor, then he or she will also be risking unrealized profit. This is a very important concept to grasp. If there is profit on the table waiting to be actualized, then it is at risk.

Person B also clearly understood how likely it was for the position to be profitable. An 85 percent hit rate may sound absurd, but that is exactly how often phase 3's of a hyperwave will enter a phase 4. This is the main reason why we say that buying phase 3 of a hyperwave is the ideal entry.

There are very few patterns or indicators that even come close to being this reliable, but they are out there, including the following:

- Three white soldiers lead to a bullish reversal 82 percent of the time[33].

---

[33] Bulkowski, T. *Bulkowski's Three White Soldiers.* Retrieved from http://thepatternsite.com/ThreeWhiteSoldiers.html

- Big W patterns meet their price target 79 percent of the time.[34]
- Bearish engulfing candlesticks lead to a reversal 79 percent of the time[35].

Hyperwave does not provide time or price targets like the large majority of other signals do. Phase 4 is the target, but that will come with varying degrees of amplitude and duration. Phase 4's will consistently garner the most returns in the shortest period of time, and this is very important. Realizing 100 percent returns in ten months is astronomically different from realizing the same returns in ten years. The shorter it takes, the more it can compound, and that makes an enormous difference over the long run.

Moral of the story is that numerous strategies will consistently beat the pants off the buying and holding strategy. We believe that hyperwave is the most effective way to accomplish this goal due to the risk-reward, strike rate, and velocity of returns. Nevertheless, we still believe that hyperwave should be complemented with a variety of tools.

When the price is at or near the phase 3 trend line, it is often a very good opportunity to enter; however, this is much easier said than done. Using complementary patterns and indicators to confirm or signal exact entry points is extremely beneficial. Just because the pattern has an 85 percent success rate does not imply that the trades in a hyperwave will carry the same percentage.

It is very possible to get stopped out in phase 3 before the asset enters phase 4, and this can happen on numerous occasions. Success rates will largely be a function of how the stop-loss is determined, what complementary indicators are used to signal entries, how the trade is managed after entering, and the amount of exposure and leverage.

---

[34] Bulkowski, T. N. (2018, November 16). *Bulkowski's Head-and-Shoulders Tops.* Retrieved from http://thepatternsite.com/hst.html

[35] Bulkowski, T. *Bulkowski's Bearish Engulfing.* Retrieved from http://thepatternsite.com/BearEngulfing.html

CHAPTER 25

STOP-LOSSES AND RISK MANAGEMENT

Think back to person B and person A. The single biggest difference between the two is the implementation of a stop-loss system. Person B religiously uses stop-losses as a way to limit the risk if a position does not go in the direction that is expected. Person A's strategy is to buy and hold with the belief that a positive rate of return is only a matter of time.

What person A fails to realize or acknowledge is that watching the unrealized profit slip through his or her fingers is only a matter of time as well.

What goes up must come down.

There are several ways to use stop-losses when trading hyperwaves, and the preferred approach will be a function of risk tolerance and investment vehicle.

Hyperwave says to hold onto long exposure until a weekly candle closes below phase 3 or phase 4. This is certainly a viable approach but may not be preferred since there is no telling how far the price can fall before closing below the phase line.

One could expect to be able to exit within approximately 5 percent of the phase line and then be rudely awakened in the event of a major sell-off. This situation is the primary reason why additional risk management tactics are preferred.

If using options, then this may not be the case because options have a built-in risk threshold which guarantees one cannot lose more than the premium plus fees. In that case it may not be necessary to implement an additional stop-loss strategy; however, options are not always the best suited for hyperwaves. That is because phase 3 and phase 4 can last for years, and most options are designed for a shorter time horizon.

Parabolic SAR

The Parabolic SAR (parabolic stop and reverse) is another very powerful indicator that was developed by Welles Wilder in the 1960s and 1970s. It can be used to time entries and exits as well as to trail stop-losses. In a study that included seventeen years of data, the Parabolic SAR showed an astounding 95 percent confidence level of being able to consistently beat the ROI of the S&P 500[36].

Long entries are signaled when a SAR on top of the price is broken. Taking profit and/or entering a short position is signaled when price breaks a SAR that is below the candle.

Parabolic SAR's on Bitcoin Weekly Chart

Parabolic SAR's can be a way to time entries into phase 3; however, that is not the case when the SAR's remain below the price throughout the entire phase 3 move. In this

---

[36] Comparison of Three Technical Trading Methods vs. Buy-and-Hold for the S&P 500 Market | Timothy C. Pistole | Graduate Student of Finance, University of Houston – Victoria

situation, some might prefer to buy right above a bullish SAR (when SAR is below the price); however, that is not necessarily what this system was designed for.

Above, we considered using Consensio to time entries. Here we can see how powerful it would be to use parabolic SAR's to time the entry at the very beginning of phase 3 as well as using them to set/trail the stop-loss. This provides an absurdly asymmetric risk-reward to the tune of 1:15 or even more. This type of setup is extremely rare in any other environment; however, when trading in a hyperwave, this is the type of risk-reward that one should strive for.

Perhaps the best part is that the Parabolic SAR's can be used very effectively to trail the stop-loss. This will protect capital and unrealized profit while allowing traders to take full advantage of the trend that is moving in his or her favor.

We want 90 percent of the cookie.

Trying to sell the exact top is a delusional and greedy approach. Instead, it is best to let the trend go for as long as it can and attempt to capitalize on 80–90 percent of the move. Trying to sell the exact top will lead to taking profit too early or holding onto the position for too long.

The best way to achieve this goal is through trailing stop-losses. During the 2017 Bitcoin hyperwave, we can see that it would have protected our entry in the $3,200 area and would not have been violated until December 18, 2017, when the price fell below $13,500. This occurred simultaneously with the weekly close below phase 4.

The exact top was at $19,672, but that is not the target. It is okay, and even necessary, to miss out on a portion of unrealized profits. It is not okay to miss out on the large majority of all the unrealized profit.

8 Percent Trailing Stop-Loss in Phase 4

A small adjustment to the Parabolic SAR trailing stop-loss system that is outlined above can be made, and it can have a significant impact on the profitability of trading hyperwaves. Once the asset enters phase 4, then the price is not expected to retrace more than 8 percent and remain in the fourth phase.

Therefore, one can use Parabolic SAR's to trail stop-losses while in phase 3 and can switch to an 8 percent trailing stop-loss after entering phase 4. Some brokers will offer an option to automatically trail the stop by a certain percentage. If that is not available, then doing it manually should only take about five minutes per week. After the weekly candle closes, then multiply the price by 0.92 and use the result to manually adjust the stop-loss.

Adding this change means that the stop-loss would have been executed on Bitcoin at $17,393.52 during the second week of December 2017. This boosts the ROI to roughly 500 percent and also ensures that the position wasn't closed prematurely.

It is almost always best not to place all the eggs in one basket. These rules are not going to work 100 percent of the time, nor should they be expected to. There will be times when the 8 percent threshold, as well as Parabolic SAR, gets violated on an intraweek basis and then the phase 4 continues and takes the price much higher. This could occur on a long wick down that closes above phase line. The weekly close below the trend line is the single most important sell signal, and it should be treated as such. This is why it is preferred to use a combination of all three approaches.

Once entered, we can use each strategy for a portion of the position. In the example outlined above, the ideal approach would be to enter 33 percent of the stop-loss on the weekly Parabolic SAR, 33 percent using the 8 percent trailing stop-loss, and save 33 percent for the weekly close below phase 4. In this situation, that would not have garnered quite as good of results as inputting 100 percent of the stop-loss at the 8 percent threshold; however, that will not always be the case. This approach will ensure that some exposure is held onto if the SAR and 8 percent stop-losses get triggered but the phase 4 remains intact.

One major moral of this story is to avoid making decisions for the entire position. Dollar-cost average in and dollar-cost average out. Enter in pieces and exit in pieces. This is almost always going to be the best approach, and that is due to psychological factors more than anything else.

Most readers have experienced the angst of deciding whether or not to buy, hold, or sell a security. The mental anguish is largely a result of trying to decide for the entire position. Instead of deciding whether or not to buy, hold, or sell 100 percent of X, change the thought process to *I am going to buy, hold, or sell 10–90 percent of X. What percentage do I feel most comfortable with?*

This change in thinking makes the decision process much less stressful, and removing emotions or anxiety from the decision-making process is a very important key to beating the markets over the long term.

CHAPTER 26

COMBINING EMOTIONAL, TECHNICAL, AND FUNDAMENTAL ANALYSIS

We believe that technical analysis (TA) is superior to fundamental analysis (FA) because all the fundamentals are baked into the technicals. If there is a bullish fundamental development, then it will show up in the technicals in the form of a price increase. If the technicals do not correspond with the fundamental development, then that means the price action is to be trusted opposed to the perception of a change in the fundamentals. The change was either already priced in or it was not as significant as it may have appeared.

Fundamental developments do not matter nearly as much as how the market reacts to them. Technicals always express the reaction of the market, and this is primarily why our default is to place them higher on the hierarchy than fundamentals.

We believe that emotional analysis (EA) can be more important than both because it is often a leading indicator. Emotions precede price fluctuations. A euphoric market will experience price increases, but only for a very limited amount of time. The longer a market is euphoric, the greater the chances of an imminent and sharp reversal. This is exemplified in phase 4 of a hyperwave as well as at the top of other types of bubbles.

Conversely the longer a market is despondent, the more likely it is to experience some extreme volatility in the near future. The market has a strong propensity to lull participants to sleep right before making a big move, as is the case in phase 1.

All three types of analysis are extremely important, and it is possible for the significance of each to fluctuate based on market conditions. This is very similar to the hierarchy of indicators in the sense that different technical tools can become more or less important at various times. The longer one's time horizon, the more important fundamental analysis becomes. On the other end of the spectrum, day traders are primarily concerned with technicals.

It is possible for longer-term investors to beat the markets through exclusively using fundamental analysis, and it is also possible for shorter-term traders to consistently beat the markets while only using technical analysis. As a general rule of thumb, the longer one's time horizon is, the more important the fundamentals become. This is primarily because large fundamental developments tend to happen over long periods of time, whereas the technicals can change in the blink of an eye.

That being said, rules are made to be broken, especially when it is simply a rule of thumb. During earnings seasons, the fundamentals can be the most important tool for both day traders and investors alike.

Fundamental analysis helps one understand if an asset is over or undervalued. TA helps to time entries and exits. Emotional analysis helps to keep a finger on the pulse of a market, which can confirm or refute the technicals and fundamentals. Implementing a balanced approach and using all three types of analysis will almost always garner better results relative to being overly reliant on one or the other. The best speculators and investors are proficient in all categories and understand that it is never wise to fully disregard one or the other.

History has shown that it is very common for the price action to diverge from the fundamentals. One of the most extreme examples of this was the dot-com bubble when web sites without revenue or profit were garnering valuations in the eight and nine figures. Understanding this drastic misevaluation would have led some investors and analysts to stay out of the market entirely or, in even more extreme circumstances, look for short selling opportunities.

By only focusing on the fundamentals, it would have been impossible to capitalize on the massive upside that occurred in the late 1990s. Implementing fundamental analysis would have shown that nearly all dot-com companies were overvalued in 1995–1998, right before most of them went on to return another 100–500 percent. Just because the fundamentals say that a company is overvalued does not mean that it will not become significantly more overvalued before the eventual correction.

This is often true; the largest gains can be way out of line with the fundamentals. Warren Buffett is perhaps the most famous value investor, and even he was unable to capitalize on the enormous run-up that occurred during the tail end of the twentieth century.

In his annual letter to investors he wrote,

> The numbers on the facing page show just how poor our 1999 record was. We had the worst absolute performance of my tenure and, compared to the S&P, the worst relative performance as well. Relative results are what concern us: Over time, bad relative numbers will produce unsatisfactory absolute results[37].

About one month before Mr. Buffett's letter to investors, Tyler could have been found jumping on his desk, overwhelmed with euphoria as a result of how well he was able to time the market through utilizing his hyperwave theory. This was the fourth bubble in a row that he was able to sell weeks before the eventual collapse (silver in 1980, Black Monday, and the Japanese equity bubble were the prior three), and it had very little to do with fundamentals.

Those who took a close enough look at the fundamentals were at a loss for words when trying to explain the rapidly increasing valuations. Conversely, those individuals who were able to focus on the technicals, while placing fundamentals in the back seat, were able to recognize the trend and capitalize handsomely on one of the biggest bull markets the world has ever seen.

---

[37] Buffett, W.E. (2000, March 1) *Chairman's Letter to Investors*. Retreived from http://www.berkshirehathaway.com/letters/1999htm.html

Growth stocks drove the price action that led to the dot-com bubble, and Mr. Buffett missed out on the party due to recognizing the folly in the underlying fundamentals as well as having a strong penchant for value stocks.

Tyler capitalized on the growth stocks during the late nineties and rotated into value stocks after the fourth phase broke down in early 2000. This is a prime example of when technicals diverge from fundamentals and why it is crucial to understand the relative importance of each.

Emotional analysis can reign supreme over technical analysis because the technicals are a reflection of the market sentiment. The emotions are what is being reflected. In other words, the technicals are a by-product of the underlying emotions.

The large majority of people make decisions based on emotions, especially as it relates to managing finances. Certain emotions, such as fear, uncertainty, or doubt, will cause people to sell. Other emotions, such as confidence, trust, and greed, will cause individuals to buy and/or hold.

People who are trading or investing in similar markets will often feel similar emotions, and this is another way to describe groupthink. Groupthink could just as easily be described as "group feel." Whether thoughts are a function of feelings or it is the other way around is unimportant. What matters is recognizing that they are inextricably intertwined.

Emotions will often lead to irrational decisions, and those decisions will be the impetus for price movement. If everyone always acted rationally, then the speculative markets would likely cease to exist.

The fundamental or technical developments are less important than how the market reacts. The market will have a significantly different reaction to fundamental developments in bear markets relative to bull markets and flat markets. This is why positive news in bear markets will have little effect on price while similar news in bull markets will tend to drive significant appreciation.

The news isn't nearly as important as the reaction of the market. The reaction will be a function of the emotions that the group is feeling. If investors lack confidence, then positive fundamental developments will be rendered nearly irrelevant. If the same positive development occurred amid a bull market, then it will elicit a much different response from the marketplace.

Emotions can be understood by analyzing the technicals; however, the latter is a lagging indicator to the former. Emotions precede price movement, and price movement is a prerequisite for technical analysis.

If one is proficient enough at emotional analysis, then there will be times when he or she can visualize technicals without even needing a price chart. A great example of this is the baseball card bubble of the 1990s.

> By the 1980s, baseball card values were rising beyond the average hobbyist's means. As prices continued to climb, <u>baseball cards were touted as a legitimate investment alternative to stocks</u>, with The Wall Street Journal referring to them as sound <u>"inflation hedges"</u> and <u>"nostalgia futures."</u> Newspapers started running feature stories with headlines such as "<u>Turning Cardboard into Cash</u> *(The Washington Post)*, "A Grand Slam Profit May Be in the Cards" *(The New York Times),* and "<u>Cards Put Gold, Stocks to Shame as Investment</u>" *(The Orange County Register).* (Dave Jamieson, *Mint Condition,* 2010)[38]

A couple of newspaper headlines can be all that one needs to see the tell-tale signs that the top of a hyperwave, or bubble, is on the horizon. This can be ascertained well before the technicals show the first signs of a reversal. Phase 3 will always have a good amount of doubters and skeptics, and those perspectives will be covered by major news outlets. A market with both bulls and bears is a healthy one.

Phase 4 will prove all the cynics incorrect, and the overwhelming majority will recede into the woodworks after the markets make them all look like fools. This is when the headlines will get so ridiculous that it is hard to believe when looking in hindsight.

---

[38] Hwang J. (2013, Feb 25). *Have Baseball Card Values Risen in 20 Years?* Retrieved from https://www.fool.com/investing/general/2013/02/25/have-baseball-card-values-risen-in-20-years-actual.aspx

Comparing baseball cards to blue-chip stocks and gold is absurd to anyone with a basic understanding of stock-to-flow ratio, which tells us that when demand increases, so will supply. Printing pictures on cardboard is not very time consuming or expensive. In these circumstances, producers are guaranteed to flood the market. This type of unfounded euphoria is a tell-tale sign that the top is approaching, or already in, and it is possible to come to this conclusion without even looking at a chart.

The inverse is also true. The markets have an uncanny way of finding a bottom shortly after the headlines are wrought with catastrophic predictions. When market participants are overwhelmed with fear, uncertainty, and doubt, then it will appear that there are no buyers of last resort or that there are not enough buyers to turn it around. This is usually when a bottom will be found, provided that the underlying asset has intrinsic value.

This is not a new phenomenon. It is commonplace in any market that experiences a bubble where the value is unquantifiable. The now infamous Mississippi bubble was very similar. Speculators bid up the value in shares of the Mississippi Company, which was stationed in France, due to the unknown amounts of gold and silver that the Europeans believed was waiting in the newfound North American continent.

As long as people waited for ships to return with the newly acquired wealth, they could not help but let their imaginations run wild. During that time, it was better for the value of the stock if no ships returned bringing new wealth into the country. Once a ship docked with less gold and silver than was expected, then it would become possible to quantify the value of the company as well as its current and future excursions. The reality will almost always be dwarfed by the imagination of speculators, which eventually causes value to respond accordingly.

In this rare situation, new wealth physically coming into the country made the whole population less wealthy because it resulted in a bubble popping that most citizens and monarchs were exposed to.

The fact that newly acquired wealth had been brought back into the country was less important than the wealth that was expected to return. In other words, the fundamentals were not nearly as important as the reaction of the market. When speculators become privy to the reality of the situation, then euphoria will be replaced with doubt and uncertainty, which will quickly give way to fear and consternation.

Recognizing these underlying emotions can help individuals to identify when a bubble is occurring, and technical analysis can help to time exits. Individuals who wait for the fundamental developments will often be left holding the bag.

Emotional, technical, and fundamental analysis are all tools that should be a part of the toolbelt. Through experience, one can understand when each tool is needed and when others should be given a backseat.

There are times when the fundamental developments are so significant that it moves to the top of the totem pole, as we discussed above. Nevertheless, this is the exception opposed to the rule.

Similarly, when there is a picture-perfect hyperwave that is clearly in phase 4, then nothing is required other than an implementation of technical analysis—in this case, hyperwave theory. One does not need to bother with analyzing emotions or fundamentals when the only thing that matters are a weekly close below a trend line, an 8 percent retrace, and/or a broken Parabolic SAR. Unfortunately, it is very rare to have a picture-perfect setup in real time; therefore, this will also be an exception to the rule.

Emotional analysis is most important when dealing in the third and fourth phases of a hyperwave. Often it can be difficult to tell when a market is still in the third phase versus already taking off into the fourth. When the sentiment remains fairly balanced between bulls and bears, then one can be fairly certain that the market is not in the fourth phase.

On the other side of the token, emotional analysis is extremely useful when a market appears to be finding a bottom in seventh phase before returning to the terminal first. If most market participants are calling for a bottom and the sentiment seems void of palpable fear, uncertainty, and doubt, then one can be equally confident that there is nothing more in the works than another bouncing dead cat.

CAPITALIZING ON THE FALLOUT

CHAPTER 27

SHORT SELLING

Throughout this book, we have focused on longing hyperwaves during phase 3 to maximize returns in a relatively short amount of time while effectively limiting risk. In this section, we will explore how to improve in every category through shorting phases 6 and 7 of a hyperwave following the phase 4 breakdown.

As we learned in the first part of this book, hyperwaves are a product of human emotion. The amount of frustration and disinterest that is experienced in phase 1, before breaking through horizontal resistance, is the primary determinant of how explosive the following move will be. This is one reason why phase 1 is so important.

The amount of doubt that is experienced in phase 2 will determine how much the asset runs away from the latecomers in phase 3. The amount of confidence that is experienced in the third phase will establish the runway for the greed and fear of missing out, which are the driving forces of phase 4.

The emotions experienced in the bear market that follow a hyperwave are an order of magnitude larger than what is felt in the bull market. This should come as no surprise since negative emotions are generally much more overwhelming than positive emotions.

We usually shy away from definitive statements, mainly because the markets are very quick to teach that humility and an open mind are essential to succeeding long term.

Socrates put it best: *knowledge is knowing that you know nothing.* There may be no better way to learn this principle than through active speculation in the financial markets. As soon as you are certain that you are right, the markets will prove you wrong.

That being said, there are a few statements that we are willing to definitively assert.

- Through disciplined money management and technical and fundamental analysis, it is possible to beat a buy-and-hold strategy over a statistically significant sample size.
- The more emotional the marketplace, the more opportunity there is to beat the market's average ROI.

A large part of timing the market boils down to monetizing emotions. Individuals who are slaves to their emotions will pay dearly when speculating, and individuals who have learned to let emotions guide, instead of control, will exploit this opportunity. The former group will never be able to beat the markets, regardless of what technical or fundamental systems that they employ, unless they can first learn how to master their emotions.

> If you want to really know yourself—I mean really know yourself,
> the good, the bad and the ugly, just become a trader. You will
> discover character flaws you never knew existed.
>
> —Peter L. Brandt

This is another reason why we believe that emotional analysis is more important than technical and fundamental analysis. Emotional analysis is about quantifying how the marketplace is feeling, and it is also about being introspective. If one can recognize when one is feeling euphoric or cathartic, then one can assume that is how the majority of the market is also feeling. Selling euphoria and buying fear is an excellent way to exploit the emotions of a marketplace.

Traders are far from the only group that has learned how to monetize emotions. Politicians are among the best at this when they take a stand against, or for, hot-button topics leading up to an election. They will use this, intentionally or not, to raise money and social status.

Another group who has mastered turning emotions into money are the organizations that advertise malnourished children and animals on television and then ask viewers to help by donating to the cause.

Comedians, actors, and athletes also do this, whether they know it or not. Most of the highest-paid professions are lucrative because of emotional monetization. People will pay to feel emotionally charged...excited...alive. Most who regularly frequent a casino understand that it is a losing proposition in the long run. However, they are willing to pay that price for the way that gambling makes them feel.

If emotions can equal money, for the properly initiated, then there is never more opportunity to capitalize than after a breakdown of phase 4. That is when emotions are the wildest, most overwhelming, and therefore most predictable.

Phase 7 is the most maniacal of all phases.

The upside is over once a weekly candle closes below phase 4. If an investor or speculator decides to hold his or her position indefinitely, then there is a high probability of it returning to phase 1. That will produce a wide spectrum of emotions and introspection.

On the bright side, it will be one of the best learning experiences that one could ever ask for, and it will present a tremendous opportunity for those who have already learned lessons the hard way. On the other hand, it can ruin anyone who chooses to follow a path of delusion instead of introspection. It certainly will ruin anyone who did not implement proper risk management.

Returning to phase 1 will not be a breakeven proposition for the large majority. Most will have bought in at phase 2 or 3. In the worst and most common situations positions were established somewhere in phase 4. If that person holds through a return to phase 1, then he or she will likely end up deeply underwater very shortly after being well into the green.

This is only possible through failing to manage the risk of principle as well as unrealized profit. This is primarily a result of the overwhelming emotions that are inherent in highly volatile markets as well as a firm belief that buying and holding is the holy grail of investing.

As lucrative as longing phase 4 is, there is often even more money to be made by shorting phases 6 and 7. This is due to them being the most objective phases to identify in real time, the risk being very well defined, the reward being extremely asymmetrical, the clearly defined profit targets, the higher relative velocity of bear markets, and the repeating nature of human emotions.

When are market participants more emotional than at the top of a bubble and immediately following the breakdown?

"It is a commonly accepted truth that stocks fall three times faster than they rise, a phenomenon usually attributed to trader psychology fearing loss of profit moreover greed[39]."

Emotions are most rampant following a phase 4 breakdown, and that is also when the markets move the fastest. This is the perfect recipe for maximizing returns in a short amount of time while also limiting risk.

Identifying phase 3 in real time is much easier said than done. Is the asset overextended from phase 2, or has it entered phase 3? This will often be a subjective gray area, and those situations are the enemy to active speculators and investors.

Phases 5, 6, and 7 are usually much more objective, especially when phase 4 is clear-cut. The lower high that phase 6 creates is usually much easier to identify than the previous phases. Placing the stop-loss above the all-time high provides a low-risk, high-reward shorting opportunity.

Tyler Jenks was often heard saying his favorite adage: "Do not tell me what to buy. Tell me when to buy it."

The inverse of that statement may be even more potent: "Do not tell me what to sell. Tell me when to sell it."

As far as hyperwaves are concerned, the time to sell is when a weekly candle closes below the phase 4 trend line. This is a basic concept, but it is well worth reiterating because it is so important. Profits will dissipate far faster than they materialized if one

---

[39] Majeure, F (2015, May 14). *Falling Knives: Do Stocks Really Drop 3 Times Faster Than They Rise?* Retrieved from https://seekingalpha.com/article/3183016-falling-knives-do-stocks-really-drop-3-times-faster-than-they-rise

is not equipped with a preemptive game plan for taking profit from a position before the market fully reverses.

Taking this saying one step further: "Do not tell me what to short. Tell me when to short it."

The time to short a hyperwave is on the phase 6 bounce and/or the beginning of the phase 7 breakdown. There are a couple of ways to approach this. Both are entirely valid, and the preferred method will have to be determined on an individual basis. Even black and white trading opportunities will often leave some room for a personal touch.

Technical analysis is an art more than it is a science.

Short Selling Phase 6

In bull markets, we like to buy dips, and in bear markets, we prefer to sell bounces. If one properly took profit in phase 5, then the only way to sell is through shorting. Closing below the phase 4 trend line indicates that the bull market is over and the bear market is starting. The sixth phase represents the ideal opportunity to sell the bounce.

As the price bounces, traders can begin to short sell, using the all-time high as the stop-loss. This approach entails starting small to retain the flexibility that is needed to add to a position if it continues to bounce. Generally, it is best to start with one-tenth to one-fourth of the desired position size. This allows us to add if the price moves against us and continues to bounce.

As price continues to climb toward phase 4's all-time high, then the short seller can continue to increase exposure. Most are familiar with dollar-cost averaging into a long position in the same manner: find a price that makes sense to enter, only enter a portion of the desired position, and then continue to build regardless of price direction. This is a great way to establish a position and starting small allows us to properly manage risk.

This principle works just the same when shorting the phase 6 bounce. The more that the price bounces, the more asymmetric the risk-reward becomes. The stop-loss and profit targets remain the same, and the closer the price gets to the stop-loss (phase 4's all-time high), the less risky it is to build a short position. Entering entails less risk as price moves closer to the stop loss. Furthermore, the potential reward continues to increase as price moves farther away from the profit target.

This is why we have a penchant for dollar-cost averaging. Risk:Reward improves as price moves against the initial entry. That being said this is a very fine balance. It can be very dangerous to overexpose oneself to a market that is moving in the wrong direction. Properly doing so requires a very well-defined stop loss, that doesn't get adjusted in real time, combined with making sure that one does not risk more than he or she can afford to lose. This can be an effective approach as long as we have a concrete stop loss and risk less than 2% of trading capital.

Short Selling Phase 7

Some individuals prefer to enter on breakouts/breakdowns instead of buying dips or selling bounces. Each approach is sound and comes with unique pros and cons. This is why individuals will need to carefully consider and experiment with each technique before deciding what is preferred.

The main reason some prefer to enter on breakouts is that they want to enter immediately before the market starts moving in their favor. Another variable is the belief that one should add to profitable positions and stay away from increasing exposure on positions that are moving against expectations.

Therefore, breakout traders will wait for phase 7 to begin before entering. This can result in a less favorable cost basis, which entails slightly more risk and slightly less potential reward; however, the strike rate will be higher and this is a tradeoff many are willing to make.

A dollar-cost average approach is still preferred; however, breakout traders will often avoid adding to losing positions like the plague and will happily add to positions that are moving in their favor.

The more this person adds, the worse his or her cost basis becomes. This is a fragile balance. If executed properly, then this can be a fair trade-off for positions that are working out in that person's favor. As mentioned above, both approaches have their merits and it will come down to an individual's disposition to determine what is preferred.

CHAPTER 28

PROFIT TARGETS

When shorting hyperwaves, the profit targets are usually just as well defined as the stop-losses, and this is another major advantage relative to longing phase 3. Hyperwave does not provide a profit target during the bull market.

When in phase 3, the target is phase 4; however, that can happen in all shapes and sizes. Therefore, it can be almost impossible to properly determine risk-reward. On the other hand, shorting phase 6 or 7 comes with clear-cut profit targets and stop-losses. This makes it very simple to calculate risk-reward and adjust exposure accordingly. The discrepancy in risk-reward should be a primary factor that determines position size. More favorable ratios should be accompanied with more exposure.

The first profit target is phase 3. The second profit target is phase 2. The final profit target is phase 1.

When price closes below phase 4, there are two areas that can defend it from returning to where it came; phase 3 and phase 2. Both areas are expected to react as strong support. If that support leads to a new all-time high, then it is classified as a funky hyperwave. Even if that doesn't happen, a strong bounce is expected after retesting this area.

The best way for short sellers to manage this situation is to take profit on phase line retests and to reopen the position as soon as a weekly candle closes below. Therefore, the plan of attack for shorting phase 7 is to

- sell the phase 6 bounce or the phase 7 breakdown
- cover when price retests phase 3
- reenter if weekly closes below phase 3
- cover when price retests phase 2
- reenter if weekly closes below phase 2
- cover when price retests phase 1

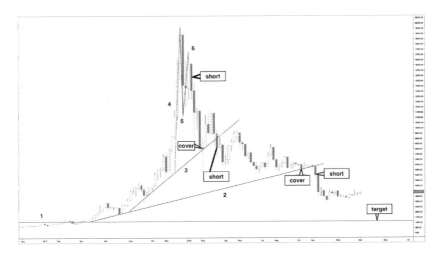

Shorting Bitcoin in Phase 7

This can be extremely difficult, if not impossible, for individuals who place fundamentals above technicals. The bottom of markets separates the true believers from the followers, and the top will separate the technical analysts from the fundamental stalwarts as well as the buy and holders.

If one believes that the fundamentals warrant the massive increase in valuations, then it will be very easy to turn a blind eye to the fact that what goes up must come down. It will also become increasingly difficult to cope with the dissonance that will result from watching the decreasing valuations if it is not coupled with a sufficient fundamental explanation.

While the price continues to fall, fundamental analysts will blame the market for being irrational if there is no fundamental development that justifies the sudden and consistent decline in price. They will likely point to all the innovations and progressions that have occurred and use that as a reason to stay resolute with their long positions that they are determined to hold.

Technical analysts can separate their fundamental beliefs from their positions. The coauthors of this book firmly believe that Bitcoin is destined for seven- or eight-figure valuations in the coming decades. However, we also chose to sell toward the end of 2017 and the beginning of 2018 when the price had only recently broken in the low five figures.

One of the coauthors went so far as to short sell his most beloved asset. This is only possible through ranking technical analysis above fundamental analysis. The large majority of market participants disregard TA and exclusively rely on FA. These individuals will be very hard-pressed to take profits when the upside is perceived to be exponentially greater than the current valuations, and they would never consider shorting without a fundamental explanation.

The only way to trade both sides of the market is through a deep trust in technical analysis.

It is hardly possible to proactively prepare for unknown fundamental developments. Furthermore, it is not possible to understand how the market will react to different events. News that appears bearish to some experts will often garner a bullish reaction from the marketplace.

Most who claim that it is impossible to *time the market* tend to maintain this impression because they are without the technical tools that are needed. The fundamentals are inextricably attached to the price, and this is the main reason why we believe technical analysis reigns supreme. Technicals always account for fundamentals, whereas the inverse is rarely true.

This perspective is what enables us to long our least favorite assets and short our most favorite *when the time is right.*

In regard to Bitcoin, the time was right to go long in the fall of 2017, take profit four to five months afterward, and then short sell weeks later. It is very easy to see this in hindsight, and the only way it would be possible to recognize in real time is through a deep understanding of technical analysis—in this case, hyperwave theory. It does not matter what one thinks about the underlying fundamentals if one knows how to navigate with the proper tools.

Those who were consumed by the fundamental aspects of Bitcoin during that time likely missed the boat on an incredible opportunity to profit. Most stayed out entirely and labeled investors as tulip buyers. On the other side of the token were the biggest believers who likely watched the profit slip right through their hands due to a belief of how high prices could climb. It is extremely important to understand the underlying fundamentals of an investment, and it is even more vital to divorce them from the technicals.

This is what will allow us to long phase 3, take profit in phase 5, and short sell it back to whence it came.

CHAPTER 29

THE SQUEEZE

Throughout this book, we have attempted to dispel several flawed axioms to open the door for an alternative perspective. Hyperwave theory hinges on the thesis that it is possible to time the market over a statistically significant period of time through the use of emotional, technical, and fundamental analysis, as well as diligent risk management.

The foundation of this text has aimed to prove that this is possible, despite tax consequences, by using real-world examples from one of the best money managers of this generation. Many approaches are capable of beating the ROI of the average index fund. We assert that hyperwave is the most effective way to accomplish this goal.

There are many reasons why we believe this: risk-reward is very asymmetrical, the strike rate is extremely high with 85 percent of phase 3's going on to complete the pattern, and velocity is at its peak, which implies minimal time commitment relative to the amount of returns. Furthermore, profit-taking and stop-loss strategies are very reliable.

The problem with hyperwaves, when it comes to trading or investing in them, is that they are very rare. This cannot be the only arrow in a trader's quiver because it is possible to go decades without finding one. Hyperwaves are a result of a macroeconomic shift, and macroeconomic shifts are rare. We are currently experiencing more hyperwaves than have ever been identified at any other point in human history. The implication follows that we are currently experiencing the largest macroeconomic shift that the world has ever experienced.

The abundant amount of active hyperwaves is fortunate for individuals who want to trade or invest in these specific types of bubbles, however the unfortunate aspect of hyperwaves is that the juice is rarely worth the squeeze from a macroeconomic perspective. Hyperwaves do not represent sustainable growth, and they almost always cause more harm than good before the cycle is complete.

Hyperwaves are a result of macroeconomic shifts, and the pattern that ensues is a result of emotions repeating themselves. As phases progress, emotions become exponentially more intense. We believe that the increasing intensity of emotions is what determines the duration, amplitude, and angle of each phase.

Phase 3 and phase 4 are driven by dopamine. Dopamine receptors have thresholds. Thresholds will vary from one person to another, but they will adhere to very similar limits. Overwhelming euphoria will often come with the side effect of greed. Market participants will become greedy about the money that they are making as well as the way that they are feeling. Once the group collectively reaches their dopamine threshold, then phase 5 is bound to take over.

The unfettered greed that has been driving the economy since 1971 is nothing new. It is a virtual inevitability for any fiat system. The high that markets are currently experiencing is at the expense of a future come down. The looming correction back to phase 1 that many major indices are facing could have disastrous socioeconomic repercussions.

Major indices returning to their respective phase 1's would be nothing short of catastrophic. We are not ignorant of this fact, however we maintain the firm disposition that things will only get worse until we take our medicine. More irresponsible government spending is not going to fix prior irresponsible government spending, it will only exacerbate the problem. The further that we kick the can down the road the more devastating the eventual fallout will be, therefore it is in our best interests to rip off the Band-Aid sooner rather than later.

A country's wealth should be determined primarily by its resources and services, it should not be a function of the fiat money supply. Money is a measuring stick that facilitates trade. More measuring sticks does not indicate more trade or more prosperity.

This is the faulty premise that our Keynesian economy is built upon. Not just the United States, but the entire world. Leaving a sound monetary standard and allowing governments to manipulate our economies has fertilized a breeding ground for the hyperwaves and bubbles that have sprung to life over the past fifty years.

Leaving the gold standard is what catapulted us into the current bubble economy. Unsustainable cycles of boom and bust are what drives the modern economy. Sooner or later the Keynesian lunacy[40] will come to a head. When that happens, it is logical to conclude that it will result in abandoning the unbacked government currencies that created this mess in the first place.

The overwhelming amount of hyperwaves that are currently active indicates that we are on the brink of an unprecedented macroeconomic shift. We believe this will result in the world returning to a sound monetary standard following the collapse of major indices back to their respective phase 1's.

We originally broke out of phase 1 when President Nixon closed the gold window, and the overwhelming amount of active hyperwaves are a direct result of the world decoupling from a sound monetary standard. If major indices do return to phase 1, as expected, then valuations would be back to what they were before the gold window was closed, which implies a return to hard money[41].

History really does have a weird way of repeating itself. If major indices enter phase 4 then we will likely see another *Roaring 20's* which would eerily be one hundred years after the boom that preceded the Great Depression.

The 1920's are the last time that we have seen an abnormal amount of active hyperwaves, which means a precedent has been set for what to expect following a prolonged parabolic run.

Returning to sound money* seems like an absurdity to most. We believe that it is inevitable. If history has taught us anything it is that fiat currencies are worthless. One

---

[40] A term coined by Bitcoin developer and author Jimmy Song: Song, J. (2018, June 18). Crypto-Keynesian Lunacy. Retrieved from https://medium.com/@jimmysong/crypto-keynesian-lunacy-16bb9193a58

[41] Hard money policies support a specie standard currency as opposed to fiat currency.

hundred percent of them eventually became worth less than the paper they were printed on. Soft money is only sustainable when there are responsible governments. History has proven that to be an oxymoron.

Drastic problems require drastic changes, and the multitude of hyperwaves that we are experiencing may only be the tremors which precede an unprecedented transformation. Tectonic shifts are occurring underneath our feet, and in the Age of Information changes are happening faster than ever before. It is impossible to know how the problem of deficit spending and worldwide fiat currency will be resolved, or the consequences that will result.

Hopefully a day of reckoning will provide the foundation for a brighter future, and that subsequent generations will look back on this century as the dark ages of finance that delivered an economic awakening. If the tremors we are currently experiencing lead to an eruption that results in major indices collapsing back to phase 1, then we believe a solution will eventually be found by returning to a sound monetary standard.

GLOSSARY

Bull/bear trap: Most understand that support and resistance will not hold forever. One will eventually break and then a big move will often follow, especially if it has held for a long period of time. Some bulls will wait for the price to break through resistance before entering. A trap occurs when price momentarily breaks through an area of resistance and then reverses shortly thereafter. This will often be represented by a wick above the resistance boundary and a body below. A bear trap occurs when the price appears to break down support.

Candlestick: Consists of a body and wicks. The body represents the open and the close. The wicks represent the intra-period price movement. The color of the body tells us how to interpret the candle. If it is green, then it opened low and closed high. If it is red, then it opened high and closed low. Hyperwave theory requires closing all long exposure when a weekly candle closes below a bullish phase line. There will be many times when the price trades below the phase line and then closes above. In this case, it would be time to hold or even buy, and it would be represented with a wick below the phase line and a body above.

Consolidation: A cool-off period that generally occurs after a large move. Sometimes the price will take two steps forward and stand still instead of taking one step back. Often the price will fit into a pattern while consolidating.

Correction: A healthy short-term countertrend move. Markets will take two steps forward and one step back. A correction is the one step back. A market that has been moving in the same direction for an extended period of time is due for a correction or possibly a full reversal.

Day Trading: Short term / high frequency trading that focuses on making multiple trades throughout a day (sometimes dozens, sometimes thousands). 1 minute to 15 minute charts are primarily used.

Dead cat bounce: Correction that occurs after a big sell-off and/or crash. The price can move in one direction for an extended period of time, but a correction is highly likely at some point. *"Even a dead cat will bounce."*

Fiat Currency: Unbacked government money

FOMO: Fear of missing out. When markets start moving fast, individuals can get lured into buying in late due to a fear of getting left behind.

Front running: This occurs when there is too much confidence in one side of the trade. In bull markets, people can become very confident in buying the pullbacks. Instead of waiting for the throwback to test prior resistance, they will start to buy slightly above. This will perpetuate, and others will buy slightly higher than that. This is frontrunning, and it can be what causes some markets to enter the next phase because people front-run the phase line, which leads to a new angle/velocity.

Measured move/profit target: Most patterns provide a price target through measuring the size of the pattern and adding it to the boundary line. Breaking the boundary line confirms the pattern and represents an area where entries can be executed using the measured move as the profit target/potential reward.

Phase line: Phase lines are trend lines that occur during a hyperwave.

Position Trading: Utilizes an even higher time frame than swing trading and will focus on capitalizing on trends that last years. Bull markets in the S&P 500 will often last in the neighborhood of ten years and position traders will try to enter in at the first few months or years and hold until the last few months or years. These cycles will be shorter in

markets that move faster, such as commodities or crypto. What separates position traders from investors is the approach to profit-taking. Investors hold through bear markets, swing traders sell high in order to realize gains and hopefully buy back lower.

Reversal: A correction in a bull market is a short-term dip in price that will generally establish a higher low in relation to the previous correction. A reversal changes the trend from a bull market to a bear market and will lead to lower highs and lower lows. Distinguishing between the two in real time is one of the most difficult parts of timing the market.

Support and resistance: Support is an area where demand has the propensity to exceed supply. Resistance is an area where supply tends to exceed demand. Identified with trend lines, moving averages, and candlesticks.

Swing Trading: Approach that focuses on taking advantage of the trends that last a few weeks to a few months. Entries and exits are much more rare for swing traders than day traders. Sometimes the former will go weeks or even months without making a trade. 4 hour to daily charts are preferred.

Trading range: This occurs when markets get stuck between two horizontal trend lines and move sideways for an extended period of time. The horizontal trend above price is resistance and the horizontal support below is support. Phase 1 is a trading range.

Trend line: A line drawn on top of highs, to illustrate resistance, or below lows to illustrate support. Can be horizontal or angular and represents direction as well as price velocity. Horizontal trend lines, as seen in phase 1, indicate a flat or ranging market. Angular trend lines show a trending market. Bullish trend lines move from the bottom left to the upper right side of the chart. Bearish trend lines start from the top left and move toward the bottom right. Steeper angles indicate a higher velocity of price movement.

Throw back/retest: When an area breaks through resistance, then that area is expected to become support. The price will have a propensity to *throw back* to that area to *retest* it for support. The prior barrier will not necessarily hold as support. That is why it is considered a test. When it does hold up, then it indicates that the market is ready for the next leg up.